PRAISE FOR WORKING WITH GEN Z

"In the wake of sweeping changes to the world of work brought on by the pandemic, recruiting and retaining top young talent is more challenging—and more critical—than ever. *Working with Gen Z* is an indispensable guide to understanding and unlocking the potential of the new generation."

—Johnny C. Taylor Jr., president and CEO, Society for Human Resources Management (SHRM)

"A new generation of workers is coming of age, with enormous potential. *Working with Gen Z* is the blueprint to getting off the sidelines and developing them into your company's next all-stars."

—Paul Epstein, former NFL and NBA executive and bestselling author of *The Power of Playing Offense*

"Whether you're in the public or private sector, the pandemic changed the way we all think about work and shaped the newest generation. *Working with Gen Z* is an essential and highly readable guide to what these changes mean for your organization and how to continue attracting and retaining the best and brightest."

—Kevin Daigle, former director of talent acquisition, U.S. Air Force

"As we reimagine a better workplace experience, supporting a robust corporate culture that seamlessly integrates the talents of the newest generation of workers is critical. Working with Gen Z provides the tools and insights to adapt and evolve as we all navigate foundational shifts in how we work and expectations about work post-pandemic."

—Janet Pogue McLaurin, global director of workplace research, Gensler

"*Working with Gen Z* is a must-read guide to understanding why building a more equitable, diverse, efficient, and inclusive workplace is the key to attracting and retaining the top talent of the next generation."

—Tricia Arneson, chief diversity and productivity officer, Yondr Group

"Gen Zers grew up very different even than Millennials. Most human resources departments don't yet understand the needs, values, and motivators of this new generation. *Working with Gen Z* is a cheat sheet to understanding how to get the most out of them."

—Katie Smith, senior vice president, human resources, Credit Union of Southern California

"Contrary to popular belief, Gen Zers are not lazy—they are largely misunderstood. *Working with Gen Z* is the key to influencing them to accept your friend request and bring new energy, enthusiasm, and fresh thinking to your organization."

—Patricia Sandoval, former leader of the high school intern program, Boeing

"Gen Z holds unlimited potential yet thinks very differently. Unlocking that potential promises remarkable benefits and advantages for all organizations, both for-profit and nonprofit. Filled with in-depth research and practical exercises, *Working with Gen Z* is the book that every business and HR leader needs in order to rethink and fully embrace this future workforce."

—Dr. Vance Nichols, head of school, Alta Loma Christian School, and professor of organizational leadership, Los Angeles Pacific University

"As an educational leader and consultant, I've had a front-row seat in the lives of Gen Zers for nearly two decades. *Working with Gen Z* is a deeply researched book that authentically captures their mindsets and values in a way that is highly insightful and useful."

—Dr. Leslie Smith, founder and president, Education Solutions: Redefined and former head of school, Orange Lutheran High School, CA

"Leading and connecting with young people today is more complicated than ever—especially with five different generations in the workforce. *Working with Gen Z* is the new bible for managing these generational differences and building the organizations of the future."

—Mike Collins, former youth pastor at Shoreline Church

an imprint of Amplify Publishing Group

amplifypublishing.com

Working with Gen Z: A Handbook to Recruit, Retain,
and Reimagine the Future Workforce after COVID-19

For more information, please contact:
Amplify Publishing Group
620 Herndon Parkway, Suite 320
Herndon, VA 20170
info@mascotbooks.com

Library of Congress Control Number: 2021923894

CPSIA Code: PRV0822A
ISBN-13: 978-1-64543-845-8

Printed in the United States

*Santor: For my favorite Baby Boomers (Mom and Dad),
and my wife and kids—Katia, Thomas, and Jamie.*

*James: To my family. Rocco (who we still miss), Fay, Paul,
Vanessa, and Noelle.*

WORKING WITH
GEN Z

**A Handbook to Recruit, Retain, and Reimagine
the Future Workforce after COVID-19**

Santor Nishizaki & James DellaNeve

an imprint of Amplify Publishing Group

CONTENTS

Foreword   1

Introduction   5

Quick Generational Facts   7
Why Is This Important?   9
Quiz: How Gen Z Are You?   10
Exercises   12

Part 1 - All About Gen Z   15

ONE The Evolution of Gen Z   17

Gen X Grows Up   18
Helicopter or Stealth-Helicopter Parenting?   27
Safe Spaces Coming Soon to a Workplace Near You   31
Conclusion   34
Exercises   34

TWO Gen Z Characteristics   35

Introduction and Gen Z Slang ("Don't Be Basic, Bruh!")   35
Growing Up More Slowly   40
  #Adulting   40
  Driving Less   41
  Declines in Various Activities   42
  Friends, Sex, and Dating   44
  Decline in Teen Pregnancies   47
  Declines in Drug and Alcohol Use   47
  Teen Employment   52
Gen Zers and Financial Issues   54

Housing   55
Attitudes about Employment   56
Health and Sleep   57
Anxiety, Loneliness, and Depression   62
Conclusion   71
Exercises   72

THREE Logging Off   73

Introduction   73
FOMO—FO "What???"   74
They're after Your Kids!   76
    Technology's Impact on Students   84
    The Science of Tech Addiction   85
What Can We Do?   100
    Mindfulness   102
    Exercise   103
    Diet   104
    Personal Connection   106
Conclusion   108
Exercises   109

Part 2 - Recruiting, Retaining,
and Reimagining the Future Workforce   111

FOUR Recruiting and Retaining Gen Z   113

Introduction   113
Recruitment and Retention ROI   114
The Four Ps of Recruitment—Getting Them
    to Accept Your Friend Request   115
    Target Market Checklist   116

Product—Job Description,
   Corporate Culture, Core Values   117
Price—Salary, Benefits, and Perks (Free Food?)   120
Promotion—Website, Social, Texts, and More   126
Place—Office, Remote, or Hybrid?   128

Retention/Turnover—Keeping Them Engaged
and Happy   132
The Importance of Diversity, Equity, and Inclusion (DEI) 138
   The Gender Gap   139
   Gender Identity   140
   Race/Ethnicity/National Origin   141
   Social Justice   144

Conclusion   145
Exercises   146
   Gen Z Recruitment Marketing Plan   146

FIVE Working with Gen Z   149

Introduction   149
Work Environment Preferences   150
   Working during and after COVID-19   150
   Gen Z Works Remotely—#Blessed?   151
   Leading through COVID-19   154
   Gen Zoomers   155
   Making a Difference—in the Workplace   158
   #AlternativeFacts   159

Gen Z Characteristics (According to Them, Not Us!) 160
   Multitasking   161
   Private   161
   Technology-Reliant   162
   Entrepreneurial   162
   Cynical   163

Training 163

Conflict, Ghosting (😦), and Cancel Culture 164

Cyberbullying 170

Gen Zers and Millennials Collide:

    Baby Boomers and Gen Xers Are ROTFL! 171

Conclusion 174

Exercises 176

SIX Leading Gen Z 179

Introduction 179

Leadership versus Management 180

Motivating Zoomers to Stay

    Logged On and Get More ❤s and 👍s 182

Holding Zoomers and Leaders Accountable 183

    Metrics-Based Accountability 189

Building Strong Relationships 192

Empower Innovation 198

Be a More "Inclusive" Leader 200

Transformational versus Transactional Leadership 205

Situational Leadership 207

Conclusion 208

Exercises 209

Closing Thoughts 213

Endnotes 217

Acknowledgments 239

FOREWORD

"We shape our tools, and then the tools shape us."
—Winston Churchill

My father was born in 1931, just a few years after television was invented. His father was ten years old in 1903 when the Wright brothers flew the first airplane and fifteen when Henry Ford introduced the Model T, the first affordable automobile. My great-grandfather was two years old in 1844 when Samuel Morse sent the first telegraph message: "What hath God wrought."

I was eight years old in 1973, when American engineer Martin Cooper invented the cell phone. Four years later, my dad bought an Apple II computer so I could learn to program. This was the beginning of the era of the personal computer. I could never have foreseen how much the development of computers and mobile phones would affect my career and my life—and the entire world.

Each successive generation has always experienced life differently from previous generations. But in the past when innovation was slow and steady, people born a decade or two apart had fairly similar life experiences.

With the acceleration of technology innovation, today's young people, born just a few years apart, grow up with very different life experiences. They use different devices and social networks and engage in different kinds of entertainment. They use completely different software applications that shape how they interact with and perceive the world.

Children today start using smartphones, tablets, touch screens, voice computing, ubiquitous social media, streaming services, and games at very early ages. You might not realize it, but my oldest daughter (a published author) tells me millions of young people are using TikTok to make fun of old people—meaning anyone over thirty.

I met Santor Nishizaki through our mutual love of helping people reach their full potential. We were both involved in Gallup's global StrengthsFinder initiative, which encourages individuals to discover and apply their strengths in their careers and in life. I admire Santor's academic credentials and classroom experience, his passion for helping people develop, and his roles as coach and teacher. He works with brilliant individuals and great organizations and is constantly discovering and sharing new and valuable insights.

Santor is an excellent choice to be your trusted adviser as you navigate the sometimes mind-spinning differences between Millennials and Gen Zers and how they show up in the workplace.

He understands people, the common differences among generations, and also how individual strengths mean that no one can or should stereotype anyone else due to their age.

Congratulations on discovering Santor's first book and the research study that fueled it.

By understanding generational differences, you can gain an advantage in both attracting talent to your organization and developing it. You'll know key strategies to use to build high-performing teams. And you might even find ways to use what you learn to build better relationships outside of the workplace.

Empathy matters. Trying to understand others matters. Study this book, and then engage with Gen Zers inside and outside of your workplace. Ask them questions, and listen. Translate the general findings from this book into personal experience with Gen Zers. Find out how they want to be seen and heard. Ask them what helps them connect to you and to your organization's mission and purpose.

Books are some of the tools we make that then shape us.

I hope you'll find this book to be a powerful tool to help you become a better leader and manager and create a workplace that is well suited to the amazing, talented, educated, skilled Gen Zers who are the future leaders of your company and the world.

Paul B. Allen
Founder, Ancestry.com
CEO, Soar.com

INTRODUCTION

You may be asking yourself, *Why would I want to read another book about generational differences? They seem to be a dime a dozen these days. Or I'm just getting used to these "Millennials" (or retiring too soon to care). Now you're telling me there is another generation called Generation Z (or Gen Z)!* Or, if you're a Millennial, you're thinking, *Finally, we get some pressure taken off of us!*

That's right! There is a new generation emerging in the workplace, and its members are graduating college and coming to an office near you. Before we start, we would like to give you some background on why this book was written.

My name is Dr. Santor Nishizaki, and I am the founder and CEO of a consulting firm that specializes in Millennial and Gen Z training to help employees be better leaders and versions of themselves. In addition, I'm a PhD and MBA professor and teach at several different universities in Southern California about leadership, soft skills, and diversity/equity/inclusion.

I received my doctorate from Pepperdine University and wrote my dissertation on Millennial work environment preferences, which has been my passion due to the way Millennials have impacted the work environment. I previously worked full-time at a Fortune 100 company while obtaining my doctorate and thought that teaching would be fun, so I taught an undergraduate course every quarter. Upon completion of my doctorate, I was shipped overseas to work on a wonderful project and lived abroad with my family for a year and a half. Upon returning to the US, I decided to pursue my Millennial dream of being my own boss and continuing my passion for teaching undergraduates what they need to know to make an impact in the workplace. But when I got back, I noticed that something was different about my students.

In my Diversity in the Workplace course, I showed a viral video from legendary business thinker Simon Sinek—author of *Start with Why*—called "Millennials in the Workplace" while we discussed generational differences, and I noticed that the classroom got eerily quiet. If you have not seen the video (put the book down and YouTube it now!), Simon discusses how technology has impacted our youth today and how they are addicted to their smartphones, prioritizing them over their friends and relationships. Smartphones are the first thing they look at in the morning and the last thing they touch before they go to bed. He also goes on to state that "there's no app" for building human relationships and job fulfillment. Lastly, he says that young people today will flake on their friends if something better comes along.[1] I was flabbergasted and thought Simon was only pointing out extreme cases the first time I saw this video, but the students looking down at the desks awkwardly and the silence in the room (as well as the conversation that followed) gave me my aha moment: Gen Z is here! (PS: Great work, Simon!)

This book will cover how Gen Z evolved into what we see today, the general characteristics of Gen Z, the impact of growing up with technology and the fear of missing out (FOMO), and best practices for recruiting and retaining Gen Z, working with Gen Z, and leading Gen Z. As you can see from its title, this book will help you be proactive and prepared, rather than reactive, as this emerging generation enters the workforce—a phenomenon similar to the time when Millennials crashed the party and flipped the workplace upside down.

Once I realized that Gen Z was here, I brought Dr. James "Rocco" DellaNeve (my dissertation committee member and professor at Pepperdine) on board, and we created a survey that was distributed nationally to multiple universities and companies in the public and private sectors. We took care to distribute it to real working Gen Zers who *actually* worked in an office—whether it be in an internship capacity or a full-time role—to ensure relevancy and authenticity. We found that a lot of existing data polled high school students about what they wanted from work. We felt that this was not a good data point because a lot changes between high school and working in an office. We are not claiming this to be the be-all and end-all study, but it gives us a first look into what the first Gen Zers want from their coworkers, companies, and leaders.

In addition, we conducted a national study during the COVID-19 pandemic to help employers understand how this event impacted this generation and how to help its members thrive in postpandemic life.

Lastly, while most of this book is tailored to how to better understand, recruit, work with, and lead Gen Z, most of the concepts in this book can be tailored to any generation to help them be better leaders and more engaged at work. We hope you enjoy this book, and we appreciate you for taking the time to read it!

QUICK GENERATIONAL FACTS

To spare you an entire chapter on how each generation grew up, prefers to work, etcetera, we decided to give you "bite-size" pieces of information in this early section about some of the ways the current generations try to coexist in peaceful harmony. The rest of the book will focus solely on Gen Z. If you'd like to learn more about the other generations, please feel free to use Google or check out my website: www.mulhollandcg.com.

1. *Work Has Shifted from a Time Mentality to a Task Mentality*

    The Greatest Generation, Baby Boomers, and some Gen Xers spent a large portion of their careers with the workplace mantra that you are paid to work eight hours a day, from Monday to Friday between 8:00 a.m. and 6:00 p.m., so you should do it without complaints or exceptions. Gen Xers and Millennials have found work to be more fluid, meaning that work can sometimes take place after leaving the office (or your Zoom/Teams meetings), on the weekends, or even on vacation, based on the timing of the "task due date" and ensuring that work-life balance is in place. The pandemic really helped accelerate this trend because as long as you had an internet connection, you were "at work."

I remember seeing Caribbean islands trying to entice people to set up their "work-from-home offices" in their countries, an offer that would most likely draw younger employees without additional life responsibilities. It will be interesting to see how companies bring back employees to the brick-and-mortar office and track the turnover rates.

2. *Work-Life Balance*

- The Baby Boomers grew up in a highly competitive atmosphere and lived their lives to climb up the corporate ladder at the expense of their health, marriages (i.e., divorce rates have doubled in the past thirty years[2]), and parenting obligations (latchkey kids).

- Gen Xers and Millennials grew up with these ambitious Baby Boomer parents, saw the toll that it took on their families, and decided that work-life balance was a necessity. They expect their workplaces—which are usually run by Boomers—to foster these ideals, which can cause a great deal of friction.

3. *Narcissism, Loners, and Micromanagers*

- Millennials can be typecast as narcissistic optimists, Gen Xers are stereotyped as being poor, cynical communicators, and Boomers are stereotyped as being self-centered micromanagers—add them all up, and you get your company's org chart!

- On the flip side, Millennials are labeled highly educated collaborators, Gen Xers are labeled no-nonsense, efficient workers, and Boomers are stereotyped as mentors, team players, and customer focused.

WHY IS THIS IMPORTANT?

Businesses and organizations spend over one trillion dollars a year on recruiting, training, and retaining the best talent in the job market to create a competitive advantage.[3] It is important that these generations harmoniously coexist in the workplace (including along the lines of race, sexual orientation, gender, etc.) to ensure maximum employee well-being and, of course, a healthy bottom line.

So how do organizations achieve generational harmony? Empathy. Think about something negative that happened to a close family member or friend. Did you put yourself in their shoes or simply show regret about that person's situation? If you chose the "shoes" option, that means that you displayed empathy. Actively listening to a person of a different generation and trying to put yourself in their shoes creates empathy and therefore gives you a different lens through which to view your "lazy" or "self-centered" coworker.

QUIZ: HOW GEN Z ARE YOU?

1. **When was Gen Z born?**
   a. 1995–2012　　b. 1997–2014
   c. 1980–1994　　d. Everyone under 40 is a Millennial!

2. **How old were you when you got your driver's license?**
   a. 16–17　　b. 18
   c. 19+　　d. Never got one

3. **Do you check your smartphone within fifteen minutes of waking up?**
   a. Yes　　b. No

4. **Your thoughts on this statement: "My employer should let me have a side gig outside of work."**
   a. Agree
   b. Disagree
   c. Side *what*?

5. **My preferred method of training (pre-post-COVID-19) is:**
   a. Face-to-face　　b. Online
   c. Face-to-face and online (hybrid)　　d. What training?

6. **Gen Zers are:**
   a. Cynical　　b. Multitaskers
   c. Hyperaware of surroundings　　d. Technology-reliant
   e. What age range is Gen Z again?

7. Do you find it acceptable to work on nights and weekends?

a. Yes   b. No

c. Only situationally   d. Is there any other way?
(not the norm)

8. What is your preferred method of communication at work (pre-post-COVID-19)?

a. Face-to-face   b. Email

c. Instant message/text   d. Phone

9. Would you ever want additional job experiences outside of what you were originally hired for?

a. Yes

b. No

c. Maybe

d. I do more than I was originally hired for (not by choice!)

10. Does the statement "If you want it done right, then do it yourself" reflect your attitude about your work?

a. Yes   b. No   c. Sometimes

11. How often should you check in with a supervisor?

a. Multiple times per day

b. Multiple times per week

c. Every other week

d. Once a month

e. During annual or semiannual performance reviews

12. What does an ideal manager look like to you?
- a. Technical expert
- b. Fair
- c. Mentoring coach
- d. Task-assigner

13. Would you want your manager to coach you based on your strengths, point out areas for improvement, or leave you alone?
- a. Strengths
- b. Weaknesses
- c. Leave me alone
- d. I have a choice?

14. How important is it for your company's leaders to have integrity?
- a. Very important
- b. Important
- c. Neutral
- d. Not that important

15. Have you ghosted (cut off all communication/ disappeared) someone at work?
- a. Yes
- b. No
- c. Huh?

EXERCISES

We created an "Exercises" section at the end of each chapter to help you apply what you learned in each chapter. This can be accessed here in the book or on our website: www.workingwithgenzbook.com.

1. List three biases or stereotypes you commonly use to refer to a particular generation (lazy, out of touch, etc.):

   _____

   _____

   _____

   _____

Now, challenge yourself to list three people outside of that generational stereotype who exhibit the same characteristics. For example, if you wrote that Millennials are lazy, remember that you know plenty of Boomers or Gen Xers who are equally lazy.

2. Write about a time in your career when generational differences had a negative or a positive impact on your career:

    Negative:

    _____

    Positive:

    _____

3. What's the primary reason you picked up this book? Please list the reasons why you picked up this book here, as well as questions you have before you start reading.

Part 1

ALL ABOUT GEN Z

ONE

THE EVOLUTION OF GEN Z

"It is a wise father that knows his own child."
—Shakespeare, *The Merchant of Venice*, Act II, Scene II

"What, do you want a trophy now?" Throughout my career, I heard complaints from older employees about "Millennials" and how they want trophies and raises immediately. It wasn't until I started studying generational differences in my doctoral program that I came to realize that parenting influences our behavior, even at work (you don't need a doctorate to realize that, but it helps put it into perspective, right?). Most of the people who complained about "those Millennials" were Baby Boomers who still paid their kids' cell phone bills, let them live at home, and helped them register for their college classes. Personally, I remember getting participation trophies when I was a kid. But I didn't see any parents getting upset about this ritual, and it continues to this day. Also, one of the common themes of my childhood (and something recommended by parental experts at the time) was that my parents said they believed in me and that I could do anything! Unfortunately, that is not how the world works, and a lot of folks from my generation were very surprised when they entered the workplace and were told that they were not special and they'd better get their act together (insert snowflake meme here).

Our latest generation is commonly referred to as Gen Z. Most demographers agree that this moniker describes those born between 1995 and 2012. As they enter the workplace, their impact is already being felt, and older generations of Millennials, Gen Xers, and Boomers are adjusting to this new generation. Corporate marketers are trying to understand this generation, which has a spending power of $143 billion. Yet in order to understand Gen Z, one must understand Gen X—their parents.

GEN X GROWS UP

Gen X could have been called Generation *I* (invisible) or Generation *L* (lost). Others have called them the unsung generation, as they were born between the Millennials and the Boomers. They were born living in the shadow of the Boomers. As the Boomers were the children of the Greatest Generation, which fought in World War II, Gen X is perhaps best known for what it is not. The Boomers experienced the sexual revolution, the civil rights movement, and the Vietnam War and were known as the "Me Generation." There were seventy-six million Boomers versus fifty-one million Gen Xers. The Gen X mentality is best described as a survival mentality. The Gen Xers experienced globalization, economic downturns, Watergate, the fall of the Berlin Wall, and rising divorce rates resulting in neighborhoods full of tough-skinned latchkey kids who grew up in an environment lacking security at home or, broadly, in a more globalized and less-forgiving world. According to Corey Seemiller, a professor at Ohio's Wright State University who has conducted research on Gen Z and written several books on its short history, "Gen X is raising Gen Z to look like them: autonomous, cynical, [and] with looser reins." She added, "They figure things out themselves."[1]

In a survey by Pew Research, Gen Xers listed these events as the ones that most profoundly affected America in their lifetimes:

1975	The tech boom	2001	September 11
1986	The *Challenger* explosion	2001	Iraq/Afghanistan wars
1989	Berlin Wall falls/Cold War ends	2005	Hurricane Katrina
1990	Gulf War	2009	Obama presidency
1995	Oklahoma City bombing	2015	Same-sex marriage ruling
1999	Columbine shooting	2015	Pulse nightclub shooting

Figure 1: Major events in the lives of Gen Xers
(Pew Research Center, 2016)[2]

While research by a high-quality group such as Pew Research has not been performed for Gen Z's historic moments, I will posit a list:

2009	Obama presidency	2019	Greta Thunberg speech at the UN
2012	Sandy Hook Elementary School shooting	2020	COVID-19 pandemic
		2020	George Floyd's murder
2015	Same-sex marriage ruling		

Time will tell which events will occupy the memories of Gen Z. Here's a narrative from a Gen Xer we'll call Bob: Bob grew up in the Buffalo area. His dad would take him and his brother, alternating between the two, to Buffalo Bills games in the late 1960s and early 1970s. The games were played at War Memorial Stadium, which was opened in 1938 and was built by the Works Progress Administration. The stadium was affectionately called the "Rockpile" due to its dilapidated condition. Cracked concrete was everywhere, and it was nothing like the modern and comfortable stadiums of today. It was nearly an all-male affair, especially in the winter. "When we would get to our seats, we would have to brush the snow off of the seats and stamp down the one or two feet of snow so that we could stand. The stadium was run-down, and so were the neighborhoods surrounding it." Bob was just a boy, but he was seeing the beginning of what was to be known later as a Rust Belt city.

The Rust Belt is a phenomenon of deindustrialization that began in the 1960s and continued through to the 1990s. It largely affected the Great Lakes region, central New York, Pennsylvania, Ohio, West Virginia, Kentucky, Indiana, Illinois, and Michigan. It was characterized by the loss of manufacturing jobs in steel, auto, and coal, which led to deindustrialization, economic decline, population loss, and urban decay (see Figure 2 for four Rust Belt city population declines).

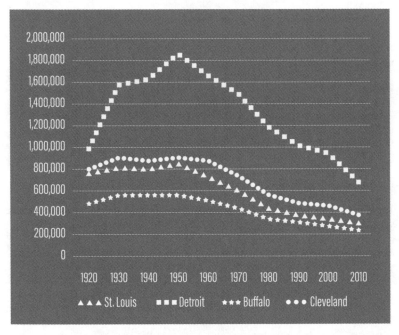

Figure 2: Population decline due to economic devastation in selected cities (US Census records)[3]

Twenty-somethings entering the workplace in the 1980s were doing so amid high inflation and high interest rates, which made credit difficult to obtain for employers. The oil shock prices of 1979 and 1980 drove the consumer price index, which equated to higher-priced goods for the average American. Due to this terrible economy, the auto industry shed hundreds of thousands of jobs in 1980, and the nation's unemployment rate rose above 8%. In order to reduce inflation, the Federal Reserve increased interest rates,[4] which made things more difficult for the goods-producing sectors, where 90% of all job losses occurred.[5]

Gen Xers grew up in an age of downsizing. Their attitude toward life was developed as they watched the negative effects on their parents, relatives, and communities of this downsizing: everyone needed to look out for themselves. This created a generation of corporate nomads, jumping from one job to another. Bob from Buffalo watched his dad—who was a draftsman—move from job to job as the firms that he worked for closed their doors or shrank their workforces. One day his dad would be home, and his mom would be typing three or four resumes at a time with carbon paper between the pages. Within a few days, his dad would start another job at a different company.

This survival instinct made Gen Xers reliant on their own skills, and the best way to develop these is through real jobs. This instinct has been transferred to their Gen Z children and can be seen in the increase in the rate of students working apprenticeships (this includes blue-collar apprenticeships), from 130,000 in 2011 to 250,000 in 2019. The COVID-19 pandemic caused a 12% decline to 220,000 for 2020.[6] Since Gen X witnessed the decline of lucrative blue-collar jobs, the attainment of a college degree became important, and they instilled this view in their Gen Z children. According to Pew Research, this cohort is far more likely to live with a parent with a college degree than the Boomer-raised Millennials.[7]

Gen Xers have been described as independent, as they were born into challenging economic conditions and were latchkey kids. Some experienced extended adolescence, leaving home but needing to come back after encountering difficult economic conditions. Many Gen

Xers defined maturity as a hesitance to commit to marriage due to their experiences of rising divorce rates in society, a trend that began during their childhoods, while Boomers believed that with hard work one could create a better life for themselves and their family. Xers grew up in a time in which their battles were fought in American cities like Detroit, Pittsburgh, Buffalo, and Cleveland. Comedian Dennis Miller said this about Gen X: "It's no wonder Xers are angst-ridden and rudderless. They feel America's greatness has passed. They got to the cocktail party twenty minutes too late, and all that's left are those little hot dog wieners and a half-empty bottle of Zima."[8]

Gen Xers' attitudes toward work were influenced by their parents. Their parents devoted their lives to the religion of work, spending weekends and evenings at the office, bringing projects home, and expending all of their energy and attention on work issues. While the Boomers felt that work equaled self-fulfillment, in the eyes of many Xers, their parents "lived to work," which looked like workaholism and made it seem to their kids that their self-worth was based on their success on the job. They observed the high price that their parents paid for success at work—stress and health problems, divorce, and drug and alcohol issues. It appeared to Gen Xers that the companies did not appreciate all of their parents' time, energy, and efforts. As a result, Gen X is committed to more work-life balance and would rather "work to live."

Bob from Buffalo saw this phenomenon with his dad. "When my dad was a contract engineer, he would be notified that he was laid off after lunch on Friday. The thinking was that he and the others would not work as hard if they were notified with more than four hours' notice. I watched company after company treat their employees as expendable. Since everyone was downsizing, no companies needed to treat their employees well. There were ten people available for every available job. You had to know someone to get a part-time minimum-wage job ($3.10 per hour in 1980)."

Gen Zers do not expect to stay employed by a single firm for their entire careers. Based on our national survey, 71% of Gen Zers expect to change jobs at least three times in their careers, and 20% expect to change jobs six times or more. Only 29% expect to work at two or fewer jobs throughout their careers.

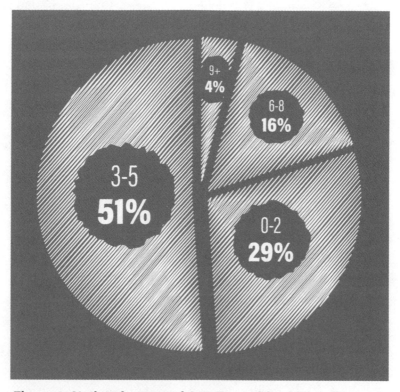

Figure 3: National survey of Gen Zers with white-collar work experience on their expectations of years staying employed with a single firm (Nishizaki/DellaNeve)[9]

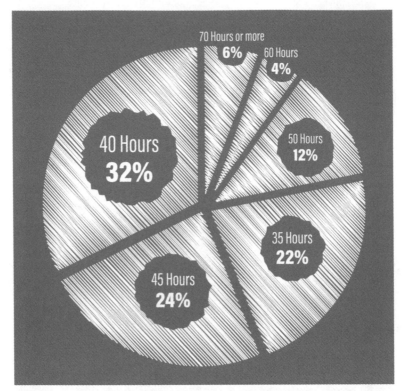

Figure 4: National survey of Gen Zers with white-collar work experience on preferred work hours per week
(Nishizaki/DellaNeve)[10]

Gen Xers experienced economic difficulties from the Great Recession of 2007. Between 2007 and 2016, the net worth of Gen X households declined 38%, compared to 26% for Boomers and 14% for Traditionals. Traditionals, who were born between 1927 and 1946, are also known as the Silent Generation because children of this era were expected to be seen and not heard. The Great Recession began in December 2007 and ended in June 2009. During the downturn, Gen X homeowners experienced the greatest decline in home equity, at 43%. As stock prices plunged, so did their financial holdings. However, just as Gen Xers saw the largest decline, they saw the largest bounce-back in the recovery. Since 2010, Gen Xers have seen their net worth grow 115%.[11]

Gen Zers have likely been paying attention to the struggles of their parents. According to multiple surveys and articles, this cohort is already thinking about retirement. The range of those either thinking about, planning for, or already saving for retirement is approximately between 50% and 75%.

According to a national survey, Gen Zers have also embraced the "work to live" attitude—78% of those surveyed desire to work between 35 and 45 hours per week.[12] Although Gen Zers don't want to work a steady diet of long hours, they are willing to work weekends if required. According to our national survey, two-thirds of Gen Zers would be willing to work nights and weekends.[13]

As a result of rising divorce rates, more women entered the workforce in the 1970s and 1980s. As children, Gen Xers found themselves in situations without parents. Working mothers make up a significant part of the labor force, accounting for nearly one-third (32%) of all employed women.

"There were around 23.5 million employed women with children under the age of 18 and nearly two-thirds worked full-time, year-round," according to the U.S. Census Bureau's 2018 American Community Survey (ACS).[14]

The term *latchkey kid* first appeared in the 1940s and described young children taking care of themselves while Dad was off to war and Mom went off to work. The description was apt for children who walked to and from school with their house keys around their necks on a string.

The effects of being a latchkey kid differ with age. For those younger than ten, loneliness, boredom, and fear are most common. Other effects include susceptibility to peer pressure, alcohol and drug abuse, sexual promiscuity, smoking, and difficulty adapting to new situations. One study found children left home alone for more than three hours per day reported higher levels of behavioral problems, including higher rates of depression and lower levels of self-esteem. There was a significant difference between children from different socioeconomic backgrounds. Children from lower-income families were found to be associated with greater external behavior issues like conduct disorders, hyperactivity, and academic problems, while those from middle-class and upper-class families did not show the effects of being home without adult supervision.

Gen Xers became accustomed to being alone, and some experienced feelings of abandonment that shaped their psyches. They yearned for attention. The concept of "quality time" was discussed much in the media, but for many Gen Xers, the term rang hollow as parents came home late for dinner, worked weekends, and found little time for Little League games and real connection with their children. Many Gen Xers felt that they came last, behind the business of work and life. As a result of these experiences, Gen Xers are seeking a sense of family. Because of the absence of a parent or parents, they have learned to create a surrogate family by assembling a close circle of friends. One can see this on the popular sitcom *Friends*, in which three single women and three single men, all in their late twenties to early thirties, navigate young adulthood. They became fast friends and partook in comedic themes and situations.

The extent to which the latchkey experience affects Gen Z at work is impossible to know, but the downward trend in the percentage of children raised in a latchkey manner is a positive indicator.

- There was a 5% decline (from 2005 to 2015) in eighth and tenth graders who spent time at home with no adult present.

- Since afterschool program legislation was passed in 1998, the percentage of children from single-parent families going home alone declined from 24% to 14%, and the percentage of children from married couples going home alone declined from 20% to 15%. Although these declines continued, according to Census data in 2011, more than four million children were left without supervision for more than six hours.[15]

HELICOPTER OR STEALTH-HELICOPTER PARENTING?

Baby Boomers and Gen Xers grew up at a time of rising crime rates and mayhem. From the 1950s to the 1970s, the murder rate in the US increased approximately 76%, and overall crime increased 193%.[16] Six-year-old Etan Patz was abducted on May 25, 1979, and became the first boy to have his face appear on a milk carton in 1984. Concerned parents pushed for a nationwide program, and this became the Missing Children Milk Carton Program. The controversial program was short-lived and ended in 1988. While it did raise public awareness, there was not much evidence that it reunited missing children with their parents.

Another high-profile abduction case occurred in 1981, when seven-year-old Adam Walsh was kidnapped in a Sears department store and murdered. Prompted by his tragic death, his father John Walsh created and hosted the TV show *America's Most Wanted* in 1988. On the heels of these high-profile cases, advocacy groups like the National Child Safety Council sprang up, and the FBI created a new agency, the National Center for Missing and Exploited Children (NCMEC). The creation of these groups, combined with national media attention, led to increased efforts to combat "child-snatching."

In 2007 there were 518 records entered in the NCMEC database as Abducted by a Stranger, 299,787 entered as Runaway, and 2,919 entered as Abducted by Noncustodial Parent. Family abduction is the taking or concealing of a child under the age of seventeen against the person's legal rights. Only 518 nonfamily members committed abductions out of the 1,435 kidnappings.[17] A stranger abduction, also known as a nonfamily abduction, is the result of a stranger taking or luring a child under the age of seventeen. Despite the prevalence of family abductions, abductions by strangers are what strike fear into the hearts of parents. While all crime was drastically reduced by 2013, the overall fear of crime did not diminish, and "new habits of fearful parenting seem to have become the new national norm,"[18] according to social psychologist, author, and NYU professor Jonathan Haidt and lawyer and bestselling author and president and CEO of the Foundation for Individual Rights (FIRE) Greg Lukianoff.

While the actual threats to safety have drastically diminished, the fear of these threats has not diminished. Haidt and Lukianoff have used the term "Safetyism," which they define as "creeping" the scope of physical safety to include the avoidance of emotional discomfort in a culture that encourages people to systematically protect one another from the very experiences embedded in daily life. Gen Xers have lived through an increase and decrease in violence, but their psyches have not adapted to or acknowledged the drastic improvements in our largely safe society. How did these improvements affect their parenting style toward their Gen Z children?

One of the key areas of departure from previous generations is the loss of children's unsupervised playtime, exploration, and conflict resolution (without adult intervention). This may have taught them to seek authority figures to solve problems and shield them from discomfort, a condition sociologists call "moral dependency."[19]

While previous generations were allowed to do things like walk to the bus stop alone and ride their bikes until sundown, Gen Zers have been locked into organized and supervised activities. I am a Boomer/Xer, and our high school had a rifle range in the basement of the school. This was in suburban New York State. The school had an active rifle range club for decades, and no one was killed or wounded. Can anyone imagine a high school with a rifle range in today's society?

Many articles have been written about "helicopter parenting"—perhaps the best way to describe it is "hyperinvolvement in a child's life." This form of parenting is a supportive approach, but it may yield unexpected results. There are multiple reasons for a parent to engage in this parenting style—fears about their child's future, anxiety about their child's safety or emotional well-being, looking for a sense of purpose through parenting, overcompensating for their own history or past, or peer pressure from other parents. These parents may contact college professors about poor grades, or they may intervene in disagreements with their children's friends, coworkers, or employers. One Gen X parent recalled a time that her daughter was having difficulties in a relationship with her boyfriend and his helicopter mom commenced texting with the parent about the relationship.

One educator labeled the Gen X parent a "stealth-fighter parent," one who allowed many things to go until a threshold was passed, at which point they struck rapidly, with force and with no warning.[20] When these "security moms" and "committed dads" are fully roused, they can be even more attached, protective, and interventionist than Boomers were. Web junkies, they will monitor Edline and Blackboard sites nightly, send emails to school board members, trade advice on blogs, and look up teacher credentials. Flex workers, they will juggle schedules to monitor their kids' activities in person. Speedy multitaskers, they will quickly switch their kids into—or take them out of—any situation according to their assessment of their youngsters' interests.

How can this phenomenon manifest itself in a child's life? Which is the better way to go—hovering like a helicopter parent or taking a free-range approach? Will the high expectations of a tiger mom make your child a winner, or is it better to take a more nurturing approach? Will an overscheduled life help prepare your child for that great college?

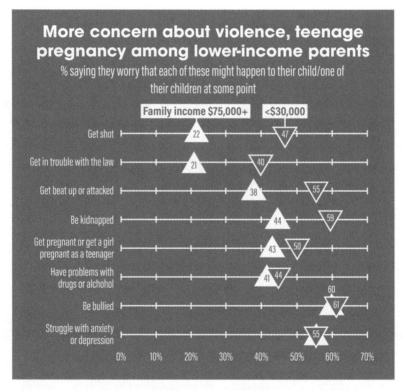

Figure 5: Stark differences in parental concerns by income
(Pew Research Center)[21]

A 2015 study conducted by Pew Research (see Figure 5) showed the concerns of parents vary according to income demographics. The great disparities in areas of concern (in descending order) involve getting shot, getting in trouble with the law, being beaten up, and being kidnapped. While both upper-income and lower-income parents are concerned about their daughters becoming pregnant, there's a 7% difference between them in this concern. Both demographics are concerned with their children being involved with drugs and alcohol, but the difference narrows to 3% more concern among lower-income parents. Both parental groups have similar concerns about their child being bullied or experiencing anxiety and depression.[22]

SAFE SPACES COMING SOON TO A WORKPLACE NEAR YOU

One of my fondest memories of orientation during freshman year at college was hearing that college is a place to hear diverse viewpoints, question your professors, and grow personally and intellectually.

The media has covered the politically charged term "safe spaces" and university censorship recently, which has caused anyone who went (or didn't go) to college to be upset about this notion of potential groupthink among the young minds of our country. Are these views accurate or unfounded?

Seeing as we've taught hundreds of undergraduate students (mainly Millennials and Gen Zers), we wanted to dig deep and give you a better idea of what a "safe space" in the classroom is and how it might translate into the workplace.

Professors Lynn Holley and Sue Steiner of Arizona State University define a safe space as a place that "allows students to feel secure enough to take risks, honestly express their views, and share and explore their knowledge, attitudes, and behaviors [*safety* in this sense does not refer to physical safety]." They go on to explain that "a classroom in which safe means no conflict and that no one is ever feeling challenged or uncomfortable is likely to be a classroom in which little learning and growth are occurring."[23]

Lukianoff and Haidt note that one of the downsides of creating a "safe place" in the university classroom is that "encouraging sharing of views may expose students to controversial or even hurtful ideas. Views that reflect underlying racist, classist, sexist, or homophobic perspectives, for example, might be important in providing the opportunity for the view holder to be challenged to increase self-awareness and to change those beliefs. However, hearing those views can be painful for students whose groups are being maligned. Thus, one student's speaking up in a safe space has the potential to seriously harm another student."[24]

In their book *The Coddling of the American Mind*, Lukianoff and Haidt state that the meaning of "safety" has expanded to include "emotional safety." They give an example of an incident from 2014 at Oberlin College in which the administration provided guidelines to faculty about the use of preferred gender pronouns in order to increase safety in the classroom. They pointed out that being mindful of a student's feelings is unrelated to putting the student in danger of being physically unsafe but can impact the amount of learning that takes place. The concept of trauma has been extended from a clinical definition to "include anything experienced by an individual as physically or emotionally harmful… with lasting adverse effects on the individual's functioning and mental, physical, social, emotional, or spiritual well-being."[25]

Holley and Steiner performed a study consisting of undergraduate and graduate students and found that the top characteristics of a "safe-space classroom" included the instructor being unbiased/nonjudgmental/open, modeling participation/developing ground rules, being comfortable with conflict/raised controversial ideas, being respectful/supportive of others' opinions, and encouraging/requiring class participation. For peers, the top priorities were trying to be open-minded; honestly sharing ideas, views, and values; actively participating in the discussion; speaking up; and being supportive of or respectful toward others.

The "unsafe classroom" was led by an instructor who was "critical toward students and chastised students or 'shot down' their ideas, biased, opinionated, and judgmental, and did not consider others' perspectives." In such a classroom, peers did not speak or were afraid to speak and were biased, judgmental, or close-minded, and the respondents themselves did not participate and were fearful, intimidated, insecure, unconfident, and vulnerable.[26]

In 2017, Van Jones, a former adviser to President Obama and political and civil rights activist, was speaking at the University of Chicago and made a compelling argument for political and ideological diversity on college campuses. He stated that young people need to be challenged in order to grow and mature and be able to make a difference in society. Jones was critical of ideological segregation and the idea of safe spaces.

> I think that's a terrible idea for the following reason: I don't want you to be safe ideologically. I don't want you to be safe emotionally. I want you to be strong. That's different. I'm not going to pave the jungle for you. Put on some boots, and learn how to deal with adversity. I'm not going to take the weights out of the gym. That's the whole point of the gym. You can't live on a campus where people say stuff that you don't like? … You are creating a kind of liberalism that the minute it crosses the street into the real world is not just useless but obnoxious and dangerous. I want you to be offended every single day on this campus. I want you to be deeply aggrieved and offended and upset and then to learn how to speak back.[27]

Whether you agree with these ideologies or not, we wanted to give you an overview of what your entry-level employees may have experienced in college that can impact the workplace. To go slightly further, workplaces are almost required to be "safe spaces" by law: sexual harassment, bullying, and racism are all prohibited behaviors in the workplace. These environments should reflect what Holley and Steiner found in their study—when having meetings or discussions, everyone should be respectful, have an open mind, and encourage others to speak up. We do not know if organizations are going to start bringing puppies and coloring books to work to help alleviate stress, but some companies have instituted mindfulness and meditation rooms.

CONCLUSION

Hopefully, by this point Gen Xers feel like they have finally gotten some attention! As you've seen, parenting plays a valuable role in how kids grow up and the types of adults they turn into. Now that you've seen the impact Gen X parenting has had on Gen Z, the next chapter will go in-depth on the outcome of this parenting: Gen Z characteristics.

EXERCISES

1. How did your parent(s) influence your work habits today?

2. Do you feel that you relate to the generation that falls within your age range (Baby Boomer, Gen X, Millennial, or Gen Z)? Why or why not?

3. How do you think Gen Zers' upbringing will shape the workplace—now and in the future (postpandemic)?

4. If you're a Millennial parent, how do you think your parenting style will impact your kids, Gen Alpha?

TWO
GEN Z CHARACTERISTICS

INTRODUCTION AND GEN Z SLANG ("DON'T BE BASIC, BRUH!")

Now that you've had a chance to see how modern parenting shaped the lives of Gen Zers, we're going to dive deeper into Gen Z's characteristics. As I always say during my training and mentioned at the beginning of this book, these are general characteristics and should never be used to stereotype an entire generation. (I'm sick of hearing that Millennials are lazy after working a sixty- to seventy-hour week while getting my doctorate on nights and weekends.)

We thought it would be fun before diving into the characteristics of Gen Z to give you a crash course on Gen Z slang. What follows are examples of common Gen Z slang as of 2020–2021.[1] Some of these terms are not new, but "their origins are much older—most [are] rooted in African American Vernacular English (AAVE),"[2] according to a *USA Today* article.

Slang Word	Definition	Use in a Sentence
Boujee	Boujee is a term that you could use to describe someone who is fancy and likes extravagant things.	"She's so boujee with all of her fancy swag."[3]
Cap/No Cap	Cap is another word for "lie." Saying "no cap" means that you aren't lying; or if you say someone is "capping," then you are saying they are lying.	"I'm actually going to be productive today, no cap." "You actually got tickets to the Bad Bunny concert? You're capping."[4]
Dank	Dank is slang for something that is excellent and of very high quality.	"Dude, that is a *dank* emblem!"[5]
Extra	Unnecessarily dramatic and over-the-top.	"She celebrated her birthday for an entire month. She's so extra."[6]
Finna	A shorter way to say, "I am going to."	"I am finna order some pizza."[7]
Periodt	A word used at the end of a sentence, meant to add emphasis to a point that has been made. It is often regarded as a more extreme or intense version of "period."	"This is the best movie of all time, and that's on periodt."[8]

Slang Word	Definition	Use in a Sentence
Snatched	When someone is fashionable or looks really good; or used to support an insult against someone who has lost an argument.	"That outfit is snatched; you look so good." "Then I said, 'By the way, everything you said and stand for is wrong, and I can't even believe people as ignorant as you exist.' Oops, snatched."[9]
Fire	Refers to something that is really cool and amazing.	"The movie was fire; you have to check it out."[10]
Shade	Can be used with its original meaning to refer to a situation in which someone illustrated sneaky actions toward someone or something.	"I see you over there throwing shade."[11]
Lit	An adjective used to describe something amazing, exciting, high-energy, or otherwise great. It can alternatively mean intoxicated or drunk.	"That party was lit."[12]

Lowkey/ Highkey	"Lowkey" means slightly, secretly, modestly, or discreetly. It's the opposite of "highkey," or when you're sincerely or assertively into something.	"I lowkey can't wait for summer to be over." "I highkey love snow."[13]
Salty	To be "salty" is to be annoyed, upset, or bitter, usually about something minor.	"I'm mad salty right now, though, lowkey."[14]
Shook	If someone is "shook," they're affected by something, usually negatively and very emotionally. It can also mean shocked, surprised, or scared.	"Can't believe how that movie ended. I'm shook."[15]
Sus	An abbreviation for "suspect" or "suspicious," so this is a flag that some drama may be going down.[16]	"I told you she'd betray you! She was always acting sus when she was around."
Tea	Gossip, "spilling the tea."	"Spill the tea— what did he say?"[17]
Thirsty	Someone is "thirsty" if they're overly eager and desperate, usually for attention, approval, or compliments.	"He's posted, like, ten selfies in the last hour. He's so thirsty."[18]

Whip	Another word for car.	"That is one nice whip you've got there. Is it a BMW?"[19]
Yeet	To throw something away with high velocity.	"Alex finishes his soda and proceeds to yeet his empty can into a trash bin."[20]
FOMO	Fear of missing out.[21]	"I'm not sure if I want to go, but I have FOMO. What if it ends up being fun?"
GOAT	Greatest of all time.[22]	"Kobe Bryant is the GOAT."
TBH	To be honest.	"TBH, I think you are amazing."[23]
TFW	That feeling when.	"TFW you have a hot cup of coffee in a quiet house."[24]
W and L	A single letter to express something. "Win" might include too many letters to type, so you can just use "W." L, on the other hand, can stand in for "loss."	"I didn't oversleep today, so that is a W." "We tried really hard in the game but still caught an L."[25]

GROWING UP MORE SLOWLY*

Gen Z is growing up more slowly than previous generations.[26] When I first read this, I was pretty shocked (and intrigued). As a geriatric Millennial, I thought of the potential tremendous impact on our society—including K–12 schools, universities, and ultimately the workplace—of the fact that Gen Zers are three years behind previous generations in their maturation.

#Adulting

People in their twenties and thirties are having trouble "adulting," or achieving financial independence, especially through the pandemic. According to a survey by the Pew Research Center, only 24% of young adults admitted being financially independent of their parents at age twenty-two or younger,[27] and a year into the pandemic, the majority of adults ages eighteen to twenty-nine said that their financial position was fair/poor (the highest percentage among all age brackets).[28]

When respondents were asked at what age a person becomes an adult, there was no strong majority.

- Younger than eighteen: 9%

- Eighteen years old: 27%

- Nineteen to twenty years old: 15%

- Twenty-one years old: 15%

- Twenty-two to twenty-four years old: 17%

- Twenty-five years old: 9%

- Older than twenty-five 6%

---

* Trigger Warning: This section talks about anxiety, depression, and suicide. Please reach out to your local mental health helpline if this could trigger you, or skip to the next section.

Those who felt like adults attributed the feeling to parents, who prepared them, and to having a job or good role models.

When respondents were asked about the definition of adulthood, 39% cited aspects of financial independence over traditional life milestones like moving out of their parents' house, getting an education, or getting married. The most-emphasized aspects of financial independence were setting aside savings, owning their own car, paying for their own cell phone, and having a job. This focus on financial issues carried itself into the voting booth, where 65% wanted to hear candidate positions on job growth and unemployment, health care, and student debt rather than on social issues.[29]

Driving Less

The digital connection enables a reduction of driving, another area of reduced adult behavior. In a world that promises autonomous cars and has driving services such as Uber and Lyft ready around the corner, is knowing how to drive at sixteen or seventeen a necessity after all? According to Gen Z parenting expert Steve Robertson, "only 71.5% of teenagers think so, a drop of more than 13% in just twenty years."[30] The University of Michigan administers the "Monitoring the Future" survey, which found there was a 10% decline between 2005 and 2015 in twelfth graders who drove at all in the past year.[31]

Many teens don't see a need to get a driver's license. They can walk to stores near their homes, and if they actually need rides, they can use mobile ride-sharing apps.[32] Some of this reduction in driving may be attributed to the regulations for obtaining a license. According to the Highway Loss Data Institute, required set periods of training and restricted driving privileges at certain ages have been most responsible for long-term reductions in teen drivers. Another factor that may be contributing to reduced teen driving is the combination of fewer jobs during the previous recession, as well as lower employment rates among Gen Zers.

Some think that the drop in interest in teen driving is due to teens' fascination with the internet and smartphones. The desire of previous generations to go to the mall is no longer present amid iTunes and Amazon.[33] In the past, private conversations were accomplished by stretching the telephone cord around the corner or meeting in person. Today most teens are connected and can have one-on-one conversations either on the cell phone or through various social media technologies. The drive to drive has diminished as digital communication has increased. Along with this drop in driving has come a decrease in participation in working for wages.

Declines in Various Activities

All of these downward indicators for destructive behaviors bode well for this cohort, but there's been a corresponding decline in nondestructive behaviors as well. Declines in more normative activities include:

- 15% for eighth, tenth, and twelfth graders for monthly in-theater movie watching (2004 to 2015)

- 15% for eighth and tenth graders attending a party at least once a month (2008 to 2015)

- 12+% for eighth, tenth, and twelfth graders in getting together with friends daily or nearly every day (2005 to 2015)

- 15% for eighth and tenth graders going to a shopping mall at least once per month (1999 to 2015)[34]

It is clear that the internet, Instagram, Snapchat, and texting have replaced seeing friends in person for Gen Zers. Online relationships have replaced offline relationships. Going to the mall and movie theaters as a social event has partly been eroded by online relationships, as well as online movie offerings and a nationwide trend of mall closures due to changing social trends and online purchasing.

Gen Z writer Jess Williams wonders whether his cohort is as boring as everyone says. Official statistics show decreases in drinking, drug use, teen pregnancy, and smoking.[35] Indeed, this generation is more at home in the bedroom than in the car or at a party.[36]

- 15% decline in eighth, tenth, and twelfth graders who go on dates (from 2004 through 2015)

- 9% decline in ninth and tenth graders who have ever had sex (from 2011 to 2015)

- 30% decline in teen birth rate, ages eighteen to nineteen (from 2007 through 2015)

- 11% decline in teen birth rate, ages fifteen to seventeen (from 2007 through 2015)

- 16% decline in going out without parents (from 2006 to 2014)

The study, which was published in the journal *Child Development*, found that teens are increasingly delaying activities that have long been seen as rites of passages into adulthood. To review, some of the key areas of decrease are among US adolescents who drink alcohol, date, have a driver's license, and work for pay.

Friends, Sex, and Dating

As they grew up during the technological renaissance, Gen Zers have the option to FaceTime, Skype, Twitch, and use other platforms to communicate with their friends rather than hop in the car and hang out. In 2015, Pew Research surveyed 1,009 teens with a close friend, defined as "someone you can talk to about things that are really important to you, but who is not a girlfriend or boyfriend." School is, by far, the top place (83%) where teens spend time with their best friends on a regular basis. Someone's house (58%) was the next most popular location for getting together but was more prevalent among wealthier and white teens, whereas boys and Black teens hung out with their closest friends in neighborhoods (42%). Online hangouts were next, at 55%, and sports, clubs, hobbies, and extracurricular activities came in at 45%. Coffee shops, malls, and stores were the sixth most popular (23%) context for meeting up with a best friend, and church, temple, or synagogue as a meeting place came in at 21%.[37]

For one eighteen-year-old Gen Zer who likes to be in front of several screens—multitasking on a work project, playing video games, and watching YouTube clips—the thought of shutting it all down for a date seems like a waste. "For an average date, you're going to spend at least two hours, and in that two hours, I won't be doing something that I enjoy," he said. He also said he has never had sex and that he'd rather be watching YouTube videos and making money. Sex, he said, "is not going to be something that people ask you for on a résumé."

An Australian study conducted in 2016 (1,285 students, grades ten through twelve) investigated the feelings of those who have not had sexual intercourse (783).[38] The feelings about this topic among students were overwhelmingly positive.

Negative feelings were not reported until the fifth characteristic.

- Good
- Happy
- Fantastic
- Proud
- Anxious

- Worried
- Embarrassed
- Upset
- Regretful
- Guilty

Students who had not had sex felt empowered:

- I am proud to say no and mean it.
- I do not feel ready to have sexual intercourse.
- I have not met a person I wanted to have intercourse with.
- I have not been in a relationship long enough.

The remaining reasons for not having sexual intercourse involved more external factors:

- My current (or most recent) partner is (was) not willing.
- Fear of pregnancy.
- I worry about contracting STIs.
- I have not had the opportunity to have sex.
- I worry about contracting HIV/AIDS.
- I am too shy or embarrassed to initiate sex with a partner.

The important conclusion of the study was that students who were not engaging in sexual intercourse were content with their current sexual circumstances, experiences, and choices. They did not feel pressure from others about their choices regarding sex, and they appeared to be managing their sexual behavior well.

Declines in dating may be a contributory factor to teens having less sex. While 15% of American adults have used online dating technology, only 8% of teens have. In a 2015 Pew Research study of 1,060 teens aged thirteen to seventeen, 64% had never been in a romantic relationship, 26% had not met a romantic partner online, and 8% had met a romantic partner online.[39] While 55% of teens said that they showed interest by flirting in person, 46% preferred to share something interesting or funny, and 31% sent flirtatious messages.

Once teens have established a relationship, nearly three-quarters of them maintain daily contact with their partner through:

- Texting: 72%

- Talking on the phone: 39%

- In person: 21%

- Social media: 21%

- Instant messaging: 29%

- Video chat: 12%

- Messaging apps: 20%

- Email: 6%

- Video games: 4%

This technology-supported dating can make teens feel more connected and closer to their partners. Or it can cause feelings of jealousy and uncertainty.

Social media makes teens feel:

- More connected to what's happening in their partner's life: 59%

- Emotionally closer to their significant other: 44%

- Jealous or unsure about their relationship: 27%

- Very jealous or unsure about their relationship: 7%

While digital platforms facilitate finding and maintaining relationships, they can also facilitate relationship breakups. Sixty-two percent of teens have broken up with someone in person, and nearly one in four (27%) have broken up with someone via text message.

Decline in Teen Pregnancies

Some good news is the positive trend in teen pregnancies. The Centers for Disease Control and Prevention shows a 57% decline in teen births in mothers aged ten to fourteen from 2000 to 2016.[40] The Guttmacher Institute could not attribute the trend of declining birth rate directly to any specific intervention but noted that this falling rate of sexual activity among ninth and tenth graders was encouraging. A study published in 2017 by the journal *Psychological Science* found that the more teens were exposed to sexual content in movies, the earlier they started having sex.[41] We do know that amid exposure to pornography and other sexually explicit material, this effect seems to run counter to the steep decline in self-reported sexual activity.

Declines in Drug and Alcohol Use

The US Department of Health has released figures that reveal a decrease in drinking, drug use, smoking, and pregnancy among teenagers. Gen Zers are more comfortable in their bedrooms than in a car or at a party, and they are physically safer than teens have ever been.[42] They are less likely to get into a car accident and—having less of a taste for alcohol than their predecessors—are less susceptible to drinking's attendant ills (very good things). As with a reduction in delinquency, truancy, and promiscuity, alcohol abuse is down to levels not seen since the 1950s.[43] One could say that we should be celebrating Gen Zers' good judgment and self-control as well as extolling their parents and teachers.

These reductions in alcohol have been mirrored by a reduction in the use of illicit drugs and marijuana. Since 1993 the drop in alcohol use has been precipitous—approximately 33%. From 2008 to 2015, there was a 16% decline in eighth and tenth graders who had tried alcohol. There was a 9% decline for twelfth graders from 2011 through 2015. Binge drinking among twelfth graders declined 12% from 2005 through 2015. However, there has been an approximately 7% increase in illicit drug use among eighteen-, twenty-one-, and twenty-two-year-olds since 2008.[44]

These reductions in alcohol use contributed to a marked decline in car accidents when comparing Gen Z to their Millennial and Gen X counterparts. A similar decline was seen in a large study done by the European Public Health Association. Of the twenty-eight countries studied (the subjects were eleven-, thirteen-, and fifteen-year-olds measured in 2002, 2006, and 2010), twenty showed a clear downward trend in weekly alcohol use. Eastern European countries showed slight increases between 2002 and 2006 but decreased substantially from 2006 to 2010.[45]

There have been impressive developments related to crime. Prior to the recent rise in 2020, it was well known that crime was down. In fact, from 1994 to 2019, there was an approximately 74% drop in arrests for serious violent offenses by juveniles (see Figure 7).[46] Juvenile arrests receded faster in that time span than adult arrests, and property and violent crime arrests of youths also had sunk to its lowest point in twenty-five years. (See Figure 6 for overall juvenile arrests.)

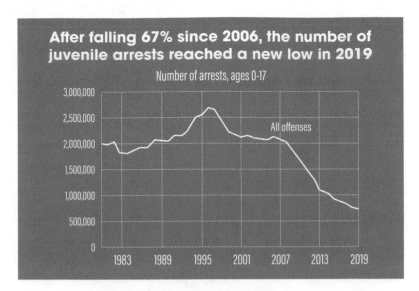

Figure 6: Overall number of juvenile arrests

(Office of Juvenile Justice and Delinquency Prevention)[47]

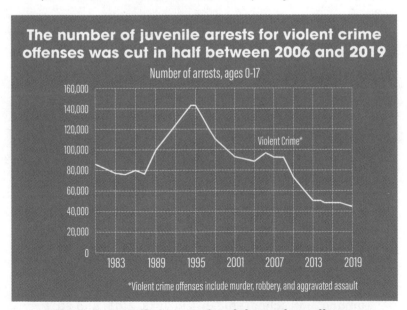

Figure 7: Juvenile arrests for violent crime offenses

(Office of Juvenile Justice and Delinquency Prevention)[48]

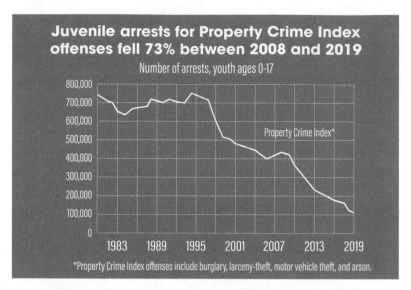

Figure 8: Juvenile arrests for property crime offenses
(Office of Juvenile Justice and Delinquency Prevention)[49]

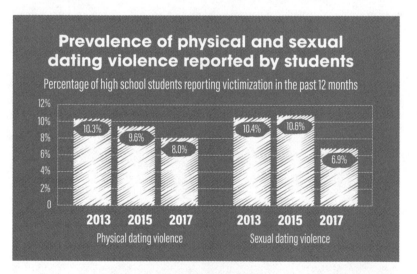

**Figure 9: Decline in physical and sexual dating violence
among high school students in 2013, 2015, and 2017**
(Office of Juvenile Justice and Delinquency Prevention)[50]

Although rape rates are far too high, they have been decreasing among college and high school youths. Between 2013 to 2017, there was an approximately 3% drop in sexual and dating violence (see Figure 9).[51] Headlines across the US carried the news that on US college campuses, "one in five women are victims of completed or attempted sexual assault." The data from various studies are wildly divergent. A US Department of Justice special report on female victims of sexual violence between 1994 to 2010 showed a 64% decline, from 5 per 1,000 to 1.8 per 1,000[52] (see Figure 10). Another Department of Justice report on violent victimization of college students from 1995 to 2002 showed a 23% decline in rape and sexual assaults for students and a 7% decline for nonstudents.[53] Although the data from these studies are divergent, both show a decline.

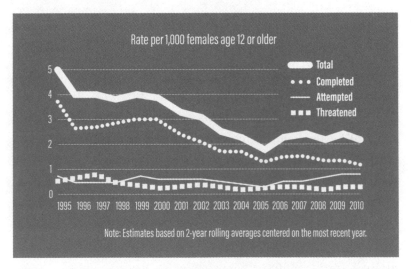

Figure 10: Rape and sexual assault victimization rates among females, 1994–2010 (US Department of Justice)[54]

Teen Employment

The employment effects of the Great Recession have faded, but only 55% of today's high school seniors have jobs when school is in session, compared to 77% during the late 1970s.[55] In fact, the US unemployment rate has declined to record lows (under 4% by 2018), but employment participation by Gen Z is still in decline. Historically teen participation rates decline during recessions and have done so for thirty years. Gen Zers are less likely to be working than previous generations when they were teens and young adults. Only 18% of Gen Z teens (ages fifteen to seventeen) were employed in 2018, compared with 27% of Millennial teens in 2002 and 41% of Gen Xers in 1986. Among young adults ages eighteen to twenty-two, only 62% of Gen Zers were employed in 2018 compared to 71% for Millennials and 79% for Gen Xers at a comparable age. Overall, summer job participation among teens in 2017 was 27% lower than in 1989.[56]

Teens who want to work are going to find challenges. First, there are fewer jobs available in the sectors that historically have been friendly to hiring inexperienced workers. The retail sector has shuttered stores by the thousands as the shift to online shopping increases and older workers compete for fast-food jobs. According to a 2020 Pew Research study, Gen Zers are less likely to work compared to previous generations at the same age.[57] Their research found that among fifteen- to seventeen-year-olds the percentage of civilians who were employed during the prior year has decreased significantly approximately every fifteen years since 1968:

- 2018: 19%
- 2002: 30%

- 1986: 41%
- 1968: 48%

Among eighteen- to twenty-one-year-olds, the percentage of civilians who were employed during the prior year has decreased significantly approximately every fifteen years since 1968:

- 2018: 58%
- 2002: 72%

- 1986: 78%
- 1968: 80%

Parental pressure on teens to have a job has lessened with time as well. Parents see other activities as capable of creating value for their children, including those that help build a profile for the best colleges and universities. New, high-value opportunities are also being created by tech companies like Microsoft, Google, and Facebook. Facebook has a program partnership with the nonprofit Foundation for a College Education that welcomes students living near the Menlo Park, California, headquarters. The program runs for six weeks and targets students from underprivileged backgrounds. Google has its Computer Science Summer Institute, which runs in the summer months. Microsoft has six-week internship programs for digital art programming and gaming, as well as three-day high school boot camps for those pursuing STEM (science, technology, engineering, and mathematics).[58] These high-value opportunities are replacing traditional summer jobs and can be seen as a positive response to the lower work-participation rates.

These lower work-participation rates are not to be confused with motivation to work. The best explanation for the drop in teenage labor participation is education. Teens are remaining in high school longer, going to college more often, and taking more summer classes. But the trends in college attendance have been changing. The share of eighteen- to twenty-four-year-olds attending college in the US hit an all-time high in October 2008, driven by a recession-era surge in enrollments at community colleges, according to a Pew Research Center analysis of newly released data from the US Census Bureau.[59]

From 2011 to 2018, undergraduate college enrollment dropped by 1.8 million. During the same period, the number of students enrolled in two-year colleges dipped by 25%, or 1.4 million, to 4.3 million.[60]

The aftershocks of COVID-19 have exacerbated an already negative employment picture for recent college graduates. Labor participation was 87% in 2007 and 88% in 2008, at the height of the Great Recession, as compared to the COVID-19 recession labor rates of 86% in 2019 and 79% in 2020.[61]

GEN ZERS AND FINANCIAL ISSUES

A *Harvard Business Review* article by John Christianson encouraged wealthy parents to discuss with their children the financial future that the children want to achieve.[62] The salient points were listed as:

- What do you think are the most important things to our family?

- Why do you think they're important?

- What do you dream about doing or being in your life?

- How do you define success in life, work, money?

- What are you afraid of or worrying about in life, work, money?

- What subjects, activities, hobbies make you feel most alive? Joyful? Happy?

According to Christianson, "Parents should talk to their kids about family values and beliefs around money during their formative years— in an age-appropriate way. Frugality, budgets, saving, generosity, use of debt, and entrepreneurialism are all examples of money values that can be discussed and modeled in various age-appropriate ways." This is a departure from previous generations of parents, who did not talk about money or financial topics with their kids. Gen Zers' parents have taken a very different approach with their children than Baby Boomers took with Gen X, and it may represent a real shift in parenting perspective.

Such parental advice about financial matters could never account for the impact of the COVID-19 pandemic. Approximately half of nonretired adults say that the effects of the pandemic will make it harder for them to achieve their long-term financial goals. Among those who think that their financial situation has gotten worse, approximately 44% think that it will take three years or more to recover, and 10% think that they will never recover.

The financial impact of the pandemic was strongest on members of the lowest income group, who were 31% worse off (compared to the highest income group, which was only 11% worse off). Among Gen Zers and Millennials aged eighteen to twenty-nine, 37% were better off, which was the second-highest score, and 24% of those in this age group were worse off, which was near the average for all groups.[63]

HOUSING

Gen Z's attitudes toward homeownership resemble previous generations' strong support of homeownership. In a 2015 MacArthur Foundation study on housing, 70% of respondents said they aspired toward owning homes.[64] But the respondents here were asked about the challenges of homeownership under the following conditions:

- A family of four with an income of $24,000: 89% find it difficult to own a home.

- A family of four with an income of $50,000: 65% find it difficult to own a home.

- Young adults just entering the workforce: 50% find it difficult to own a home.

Multiple surveys of Millennial renters have revealed answers such as "I cannot afford" to become a homeowner. These responses come in the wake of the Great Recession and amid the presence of student loan debt, credit card debt, and higher-priced real estate in urban areas, all of which make paying rent while saving for a down payment for a mortgage unaffordable.[65]

ATTITUDES ABOUT EMPLOYMENT

Even though we're going to have an entire chapter on how to recruit and retain Gen Zers, we wanted to give you a sneak peek in this section. Gen Zers are often referred to as digital natives, and as such, the process of recruitment likely needs to change. It is a given that many firms have already switched their recruitment processes to take place primarily online. But this digitization needs to go further, as HR information processes will need to be more fully integrated and accessible to all employees, and HR departments will need to become competent at digital marketing and data analytics.

Gen Zers are accustomed to mass customized apps that can specifically target their needs. Will HR departments be able to respond to and recognize candidates' unique traits and interests? Can they use analytics to leverage data that may be able to design jobs around people instead of fitting people into jobs? Can HR professionals use data that may be richer than mere job requirements—perhaps even data that considers the "whole" person?[66]

HEALTH AND SLEEP

Parents and experts in medicine and education are concerned about the lack of sleep among members of this generation. The topic has been addressed in numerous articles with titles such as "Study or Sleep? For Better Grades Should Teens Go to Bed Early?" and "How Much Sleep Do Teens Really Need?" This sleep-loss phenomenon, which is characterized by later bedtimes and early class times, has been studied by the World Health Organization. The lack of sleep results in a "sleep debt" and is associated with impairment in areas such as school performance, driving, and several areas of cognition.[67] Homework is cited as a primary driver of sleep deprivation, and as commitments and assignments outside of school increase with age, sleep deprivation also increases.

Another factor affecting sleep is peer interaction through technology and social media. In a study performed by the Health Sciences Center of Stony Brook University, 44% of teens were found to access their phones just before bed each night.[68]

According to the American Academy of Sleep Medicine, "Poor sleep can negatively affect a student's grades, increase the odds of emotional and behavioral disturbance."[69] In other words, studies support the notion that academic performance is worsened when sleep times are shortened.

Sleep deprivation results in multiple cognitive problems that have been identified through multiple studies. Here is an abbreviated list, according to *Accident Analysis & Prevention*:

- Attention lapses

- Reduction in retention of educational content

- Reduction in mental maintenance of information

- Reduction in newly formed memories

- Increased impulsivity

- Acquisition and use of driving skills (One study of seventeen- to twenty-two-year-old US drivers who slept fewer than eight hours per night found that they were 1.28 times more likely to be involved in a motor vehicle accident than drivers who slept eight hours or more per night.[70])

The combination of technology and caffeine can hinder sleep. The bright light of display technology (e.g., phones, tablets, and laptops) has been found to dampen melatonin release, which is critical to the sleep cascade process (the functions and mechanisms that lead to sleep). One study illustrated that an hour of gaming prior to bed elicited lighter sleep cycles, which contributed to the cognitive issues shown in the previous paragraph. In a national survey of Gen Zers, 73% said that they brought their cell phones to bed, and 85% said they checked their social media before going to bed.[71]

Finally, caffeine contributes to reduced or poor sleep. With the popularity of chain coffee shops, as well as energy drinks and other caffeinated beverages, this generation is more heavily caffeinated than previous generations. A 2017 study by professors Alison Ludden (psychology, College of the Holy Cross) and Amy Wolfson (psychology, Loyola University - Maryland) showed that heavy caffeine use in adolescence was associated with increased daytime sleepiness, which led to lethargy from sleep debt and was likely combated with a dose of caffeine to complete the vicious cycle.[72]

A 2017 report by the Centers for Disease Control and Prevention showed that almost 40% of American adults and nearly 20% of adolescents are obese (obesity is medically defined as having a body mass index greater than 30)—the highest rates ever recorded for the US.[73] The obesity rates for children are:[74]

- Ages twelve through nineteen: 20.6%

- Ages six through eleven: 18.4%

- Ages two through five: 13.9%

The consequences of the obesity epidemic are tremendous. Obesity is accompanied by high blood pressure, heart disease, and stroke, which result in a massive financial burden on the US medical system. The cost is estimated at $190 billion per year in weight-related medical bills. Part of this cost will be borne by companies that hire Gen Zers.

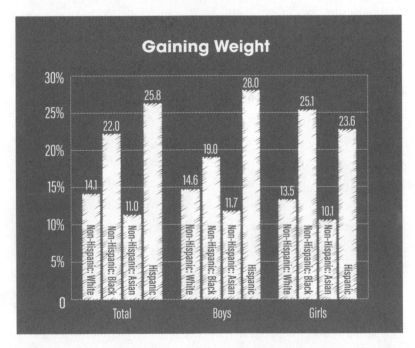

Figure 11: Prevalence of obesity among Americans aged two to nineteen years, by sex, race, and Hispanic origin (CDC)[75]

Along with the dramatic rise in obesity has come an increase in type 2 diabetes; this disease was previously called adult-onset diabetes, but with the prevalence of younger people diagnosed with diabetes, the nomenclature was revised. Type 1 diabetes is caused by an autoimmune condition that destroys the pancreas's ability to produce insulin. Patients with type 1 diabetes are required to take insulin for the remainder of their lives. Type 2 diabetes is an impairment in the way the body regulates and uses sugar (glucose) as a fuel. This condition results in too much sugar circulating in the bloodstream. Eventually, high blood sugar levels can lead to disorders such as atherosclerosis, high blood pressure, stroke, heart attack, kidney disease, eye damage, and peripheral neuropathy. Type 2 diabetes is the most common form of diabetes.

According to the Centers for Disease Control (CDC), people with insulin resistance usually have type II diabetes and, in many cases (but not all), are overweight.[76]

In the US, 29.1 million people are living with diagnosed or undiagnosed diabetes, and about 208,000 people younger than twenty years old are living with diagnosed diabetes.[77] The highest percentage of those eighteen and younger with diabetes is in the Native American community, followed by African Americans and then Hispanics. (Rates are especially high among Mexican Americans.)[78] The typical risk factors and complications from diabetes are obesity, high blood pressure, high cholesterol levels (hyperlipidemia), and high blood glucose levels (hyperglycemia).

As of 2017, the average medical expenditures for people with diagnosed diabetes were about $13,700 per year. About $7,900 of this amount was attributed to diabetes. After adjusting for age group and sex, average medical expenditures among people with diagnosed diabetes were about 2.3 times higher than expenditures for people without diabetes. A 2018 article by Andrea T. Feinberg centers on the Geisinger Health System, a health-care provider in Pennsylvania that decided to concentrate on diabetes, which affects 11.3% of the population in Pennsylvania. Part of their solution was to start a program called Fresh Food Farmacy. The main idea of the program was to prescribe fresh food for patients with diabetes. The improvements for those with type 2 diabetes included a 40% decrease in the risk of death or serious complications. Their blood glucose levels also dropped significantly, but the real impact was an 80% drop in the cost per patient. The annual cost dropped from $240,000 to $48,000 per member.[79] Firms hiring Gen Zers will have to account for similar medical costs and the higher insurance premiums that result.

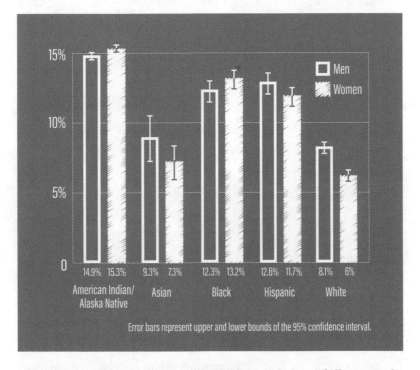

Figure 12: Estimated age-adjusted prevalence of diagnosed diabetes by race/ethnicity and sex among American adults aged more than eighteen years (CDC)[80]

A 2016 article by Jim Purcell described a ten-year study by the RAND Corporation of workplace-wellness programs that found that disease-management programs delivered an 86% reduction in health costs—$136 in savings per health-care program member.[81] Another study found that every dollar spent on wellness programs generated about $3.27 in lower medical costs and $2.73 in reduced absenteeism.[82]

ANXIETY, LONELINESS, AND DEPRESSION

In a 2017 study by the Pew Research Center, seven in ten teens say that anxiety and depression are the number one issue among their peers, followed by bullying, drug addiction, drinking alcohol, poverty, teen pregnancy, and gangs. The identification of anxiety and depression was approximately equal among the bottom, middle, and top income levels.[83]

"In a survey of eighth-, 10th- and 12th-graders conducted in May through July 2020 by the Institute for Family Studies and the Wheatley Institution, only 17% reported feeling depressed while school was in session and 20% while it was out for the summer, compared with 27% in a similar survey during the school year in 2018. Loneliness declined to 22% with school in session and rose to 27% in the summer which was a decline from 29% in 2018."[84]

Perhaps Gen Z's lack of face-to-face socialization, as well as the amount of time they spend on social media and electronic devices, is an explanation for loneliness. Perhaps the attention to technology has cut us off from human contact. According to Hunter College professor Tracy Dennis-Tiwary, this leads to the erosion of mental and physical health: "If we are looking at screens more than human faces, perhaps we are starving for real conversation and connection."[85]

Anxiety and depression are very serious psychological issues. Over the past decade, anxiety has overtaken depression as the top reason that students seek counseling.[86] A survey by the Association for University and College Counseling Center Directors revealed that 2016 marked the seventh year in a row that anxiety was the top complaint among students seeking mental health services.[87] In 2016 51% of students who visited a counseling center reported anxiety, while 41% reported depression, 34% said they had relationship concerns, and 20.5% reported issues related to suicide (see Figure 13).

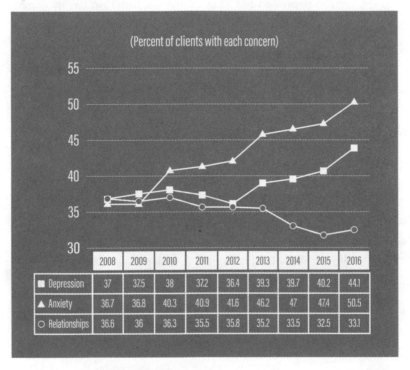

(Percent of clients with each concern)

	2008	2009	2010	2011	2012	2013	2014	2015	2016
■ Depression	37	37.5	38	37.2	36.4	39.3	39.7	40.2	44.1
▲ Anxiety	36.7	36.8	40.3	40.9	41.6	46.2	47	47.4	50.5
○ Relationships	36.6	36	36.3	35.5	35.8	35.2	33.5	32.5	33.1

Figure 13: Most frequent presenting concerns in counseling centers, 2016 (Association for University and College Counseling Center Directors)[88]

In 2007 the University of Michigan sponsored the "Healthy Minds Study," which was designed to provide data on the most effective means to invest in the mental health of college and university students.

The university continues to collect information through subsequent surveys. A summary of these surveys shows the continued decline in various emotional health issues among university students.

The number of undergraduate college students who:

- felt overwhelming anxiety has increased 6% since 2013

- felt so depressed that they could not function has increased 5% since 2013

- report emotional health below average has increased 9% since 2009

- report "felt overwhelmed" has increased 13% since 2009

- report "expected to seek personal counseling" has increased 4% since 2007

- report "felt depressed" has increased 4% since 2009[89]

In a 2017 survey of 31,463 college students by the American College Health Association, anxiety and depression far outpaced all other psychological symptoms treated by a professional within the last twelve months (see Figure 14).[90] In the same study, researchers found a statistically significant increase of 1% in suicide plans from the time period 2008 to 2016 (see Figure 15).

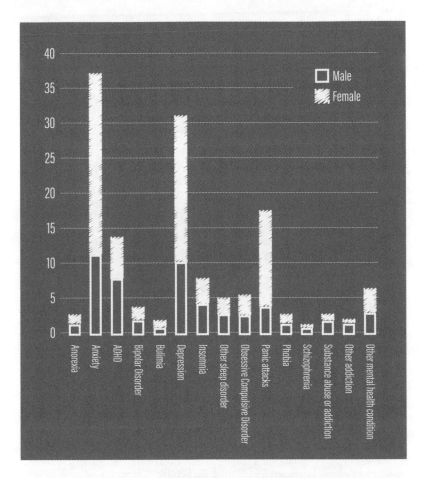

Figure 14: Students diagnosed or treated by a mental health professional within the past twelve months (2017)
(American College Health Association)[91]

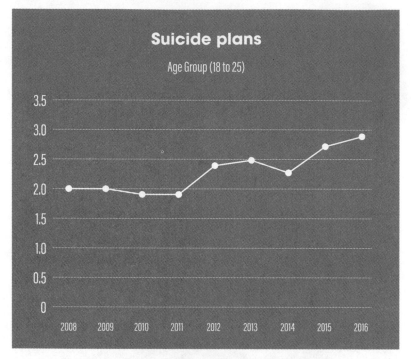

Figure 15: Suicide plans in the past year
(American College Health Association)[92]

According to the "Healthy Minds Study," among college students, there was a 4% increase in reported suicidal thoughts and a 3% increase in suicide plans between 2009 and 2017. (see Figures 16 and 17).

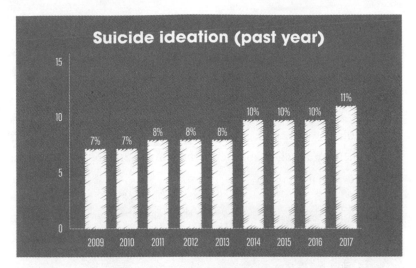

Figure 16: College-aged students experiencing suicidal ideation from 2009 through 2017
("Healthy Minds Study")[93]

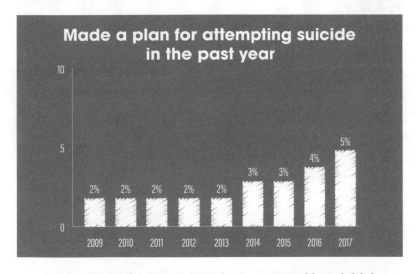

Figure 17: College-aged students engaged in suicidal planning from 2009 through 2017
("Healthy Minds Study")[94]

The "Healthy Minds Study" also found that 39% of college-aged students were experiencing a significant mental health issue.[95] Among college students, there was an 8% increase in any form of depression and a 6% rise in severe depression (see Figures 18 and 19). There was also a 9% increase in anxiety from 2013-2017 within this group (see Figure 20). These are college-aged adults, and only the youngest are within the Gen Z cohort, but the trend mirrors the increases within the broader Gen Z cohort.

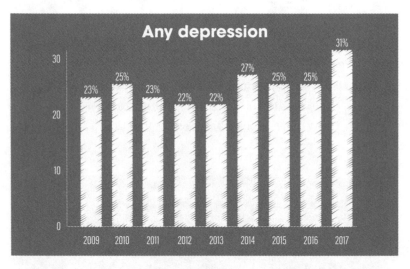

Figure 18: College-aged students experiencing any depression from 2009 through 2017
("Healthy Minds Study") [96]

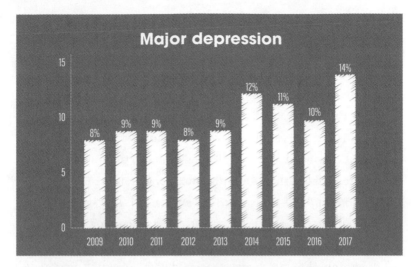

Figure 19: College-aged students experiencing major depression from 2009 through 2017

("Healthy Minds Study")[97]

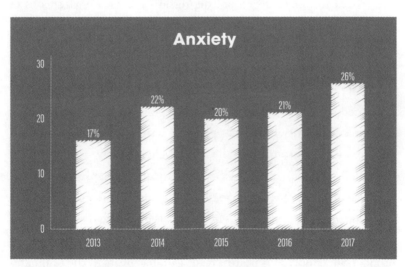

Figure 20: College-aged students experiencing anxiety from 2013 through 2017

("Healthy Minds Study")[98]

Furthermore, there is a significant relationship between social media usage and depression. A survey of 1,787 adults between the ages of nineteen and thirty-two asked about the amount of time spent on social media per day and performed a statistical analysis against depression and other factors. In the Gen Z cohort (those between the ages of nineteen and twenty-three) those who used social media more than two hours per day had a 13% higher rate of depression (43.3%) than those with less than thirty minutes per day of use (26.7%).[99]

In a longitudinal study over eleven years, 1,160 students aged ten through twenty-one were evaluated for anxiety and depression, screen time, and physical activity. The study found that higher initial symptoms of anxiety were associated with corresponding higher symptoms of depression, as well as high screen time and lower physical activity. The researchers found that, over time, anxiety increased and was related to higher degrees of depression and greater decreases in physical activity.[100] This was especially true for obese young adults. After controlling for age, ethnicity, sex, parental education, body mass index (BMI), physical activity, caloric intake, carbohydrate intake, and intake of sugar-sweetened beverages, total screen time was significantly correlated with more severe depressive symptoms.[101]

Protective theory holds that physical activity protects against depressive moods both biologically and psychologically. The biological hypothesis proposes that physical activity affects depressive moods via mechanisms such as an increase in single amino neurotransmitters (e.g., dopamine, serotonin, or adrenaline). People with depression tend to have low levels of serotonin. Physical activity also triggers endorphin production; endorphins in turn react with receptors in the brain and reduce the perception of pain in the body, as well as provide a positive feeling in the body, a positive mood, and the feeling of well-being.

The psychological hypothesis proposes that physical activity provides experiences of mastery and control, influences self-esteem, and is a distraction from everyday stressors and negative thoughts. It is also believed to improve the retrieval of positive thoughts. However, studies have shown that more frequent physical activity leads to lower rates of depression, and higher rates of depression lead to less frequent physical activity, which suggests that there may be a bidirectional relationship. It is clear that high degrees of social media use are related to a decrease in physical activity and may have an effect on Gen Zers in the area of increased incidence of anxiety and depression, which leads us to the next chapter—fear of missing out (FOMO) and the impact of technology on Gen Z (as well as the society-wide implications).

CONCLUSION

Now that you understand the general characteristics of Gen Z, you'll be able to empathize with them as they enter the workplace or attend your next socially distanced barbecue. We want to express that not all Gen Zers have the same characteristics, but these are some similarities that researchers (including the authors) have seen. In the next chapter, we're going to do a deep dive into the impact that technology has on this emerging generation and some ways to counterbalance the negative impacts of technology on Gen Z as well as society as a whole.

EXERCISES

1. Use Gen Z slang with a friend or family member today.

2. If you know someone who is a Gen Zer, do any of the characteristics discussed in this chapter align with their behavior?

3. Now that you understand Gen Z's characteristics better, what can you do to help them with "adulting"?

4. If you are a parent, how can you shape your child's life to help them grow up and be a successful and thriving adult?

THREE
LOGGING OFF

INTRODUCTION

Since I was working overseas at the time, I completely missed the Instagram and Snapchat explosion that took off in the US and was very surprised when I came back to see how many people were on their phones *all the time*. Specifically, I noticed that people were looking at their phones while pushing strollers, walking their dogs, eating at restaurants, sitting at meetings, hiking,[1] and much more. How did this happen, and what can we do to reconnect with our loved ones, friends, coworkers, and the rest of humanity? This chapter will discuss the impact of smartphones, social media, and technology on Gen Z, as well as other generations, and how we can manage our technology without letting technology manage us.

A change in behavior in our society has been established by the introduction of the smartphone. These amazingly powerful devices are 32,600 times more powerful than the computers of the Apollo space mission age.[2] Mobile access to the World Wide Web provides the user with information, media of all types, games, entertainment, communications, and social media. This computing power and information access have changed our behavior. Go to any airport terminal, and you will see upward of 80% of the passengers with their heads stooped over while they stare intently into their smartphones. Watch a group of young adults sitting together, and you'll see them individually staring at their screens. Occasionally they'll gather together to look at a particularly funny video. Go to a restaurant, and you'll see entire families sitting at the table, each member intently staring at their screen. No one is talking; it's as if they are eating alone at the table. What is most striking is the amount of time that our youngest generation has been spending on these devices. Some would say that a primary driver of this is something called fear of missing out, or FOMO.

What is the impact of spending so much time using smartphones and social media? Will it impact our families, friends, and coworkers? What can we do about it as parents and leaders? This chapter will give you a snapshot of the impact of technology on Gen Z and society as a whole and how we can maintain a healthy balance.

Note: If you need mental health support, please contact the following resources: Emergency Medical Services—911; National Suicide Prevention Lifeline, 1-800-273-TALK (8255); or SAMHSA Treatment Referral Helpline, 1-877-SAMHSA7 (1-877-726-4727).

FOMO—FO "WHAT???"

A lot has been written about our youngest generation's FOMO, and many have observed this syndrome seemingly driving them to a near addiction to the internet.[3] With the increasing use of social media over the last decade, both parents and researchers have become concerned about whether social media use is doing more harm than good.[4] Venture capitalist, writer, and speaker Patrick McGinnis, who coined the term FOMO, said, "Social media is designed to feed us filtered versions of opportunities or things that are divorced from reality. When we feel FOMO, we lose agency over our decision-making because we are reacting based on external triggers and not true internal desires."[5]

Many studies have focused on the need to belong, the strong desire for interpersonal attachments, and the fear of exclusion as powerful motivators and stressors driving Gen Z's ever-increasing engagement with social media. This has been the focus of scholarly work, and survey instruments have been developed for the topic: the Need for Popularity Scale and the Fear of Missing Out Scale (developed by Andrew K. Przybylski, Kou Murayama, Cody R. DeHaan, and Valerie Gladwell) measure levels of FOMO, while the Social Media Engagement Questionnaire measures how individuals use social media in their daily lives. Many Gen Zers whom I talk to have admitted to overspending in order to keep up with their friends' lifestyles.

Some studies have found that the use of social media benefits an individual's psychological wellbeing, including increases in social support, connectivity, and self-esteem. But online vulnerability can often include detriments to one's psychological, reputational, or physical well-being as a result of online encounters. The results showed that increased use of social networking sites was positively associated with increased exposure to online vulnerability, as well as increased FOMO. In other words, the more you use social networking sites, the greater the degree of vulnerability and the greater the extent to which you will experience FOMO. FOMO was positively associated with an increase in online self-promotion—the more FOMO you have, the more you will self-promote online. Detriments to psychological well-being will lead to increases in both FOMO and social networking site usage.

A study by Angie LeRoy (psychology, Rice University), Zachary G. Baker (healthcare policy and management, University of Minnesota, Twin Cities), and Heather Krieger (psychology, University of Houston) investigated the health consequences of FOMO according to depressive symptoms, mindful attention, and physical symptoms. Depressive symptoms were measured by statements such as "I felt that I could not shake off the blues even with help from my family and friends." This was graded on a scale of 1 (rarely or none of the time) to 4 (most or all of the time). Mindful attention was measured by such statements as "I could be experiencing some emotion and not be conscious of it until sometime later." This was scored from 1 (almost always) to 7 (almost never). Physical symptoms were recorded by a checklist of ten symptoms experienced over the previous seven days, including headaches, shortness of breath, sore throat, and chest pain. The results of the study showed FOMO was significantly associated with more depressive symptoms, more physical symptoms, and more inattentiveness.[6] We will discuss inattentiveness in greater depth as we cover the neurological aspects of technology vis-à-vis Gen Z.

THEY'RE AFTER YOUR KIDS!

There is a considerable amount of psychology involved in engineering the addictive experience into online games, social media, and shopping. Here is a much-abbreviated description of different engineered strategies:

Milestone goals—Adam Alter, a professor of marketing at New York University's Stern School of Business and *New York Times* best-selling author, uses a great example of the times run during marathons. Milestone goals set by participants show an increasing cluster of finishing times around each major increment of time. Game designers are aware of the psychology driving goals and incorporate this strategy into their game designs (hitting one hundred thousand points, etc.).[7]

1. *Streaks*—This is where hitting a specific milestone is not as important as hitting a steady stream of highs. Snapchat uses elongated red lines to display the number of days two users have interacted. This design feature is so effective that an anecdotal story reported teens asking friends to babysit their streaks while they were on vacation.

2. *Social comparison*—By comparing what you have or
    have achieved to what others have or have achieved,
    you will always suffer the sting of others who have more or
    have achieved more. Two studies investigated how social
    comparison to peers through interactions on Facebook
    might impact users' psychological health. The first study
    revealed an association between time spent on Facebook
    and depressive symptoms for both genders. However,
    when looking at time spent and making social comparisons
    through Facebook, only men showed depressive symptoms.
    The second study found that the relationship between
    the amount of time spent on Facebook and depressive
    symptoms was uniquely brought about by Facebook
    social comparisons. Both studies provide evidence that
    people feel depressed after spending a great deal of time
    on Facebook because they feel bad when comparing
    themselves to others.

3. *Feedback*—Whether on Reddit or Facebook, the lure
    of button-pushing for responses is well documented.
    Facebook has the ability to run experiments on hundreds
    of millions of its users. One experiment looked at the
    now-familiar "like" button. The introduction of this simple
    concept allowed users to gamble on seeking positive
    feedback on every post. Liking has become a form of
    social support, as well as angst, for many. This form of social
    reciprocity exerts pressure on the participant. The "like"
    apps creator posted this concerning this new concept:
    "It's our generation's crack cocaine. People are addicted.
    We experience withdrawals. We are so driven by this drug,
    getting just one hit elicits peculiar reactions. I'm talking

about Like. They've inconspicuously emerged as the first digital drug to dominate our culture."[8]

   a. *Video game feedback*—Games are designed to provide a steady dose of small rewards to keep the player engaged with the game. Moving your mouse over a box so some text will pop up, a subtle "ding" sound, a white flash. Designers include a layer of surface feedback from the game that sits above the game rules; this is not essential to the game rules but is essential to the game's success. It can be any kind of effect: candies being replaced by bricks, grass bending as a character runs through it. To date, the game Candy Crush Saga has earned around $2.5 billion.

   b. *Delay on loading Instagram or Twitter*—This creates the anticipation of "Will I win?" It stimulates the cogs on the slot machine and creates expectations.

4. *Loss disguised as a win*—This technique has been used by slot machines for decades and has carried over to online and electronic games. A typical scenario has you spinning fifteen simultaneous lines of reels. If you match all five reels on just one of fifteen, the machine will reward you with flashing lights and sound. But you lost on fourteen other lines, and if you are playing for money, you have lost some of your investment.

5. *Progress*—The common approach to game design whereby the player progresses in either level of difficulty or from simple to complex.

6. *Beginner's luck and early rewards*—A difficult game for novices will quickly end for the player and discourage

further use. The game designers quickly figured this out and ensured that a novice player could gain enjoyment from the early wins and beginner's luck, as well as suffer defeat in subsequent levels, driving the addiction for early success.

7. *Escalation*—The lure of developing mastery can drive addiction. As the challenge escalates, the player increases their abilities in order to keep pace. The term *zone of proximal development*, coined by Lev Vygotsky, differentiates between what a learner can do without aid, what they can do with guidance, and what they cannot do. The game player will drive themselves to gain ever-increasing mastery.

8. *Cliff-hanger*—These are similar to devices used in dramatic stories that hook fans with unresolved plotlines and are commonly applied to online shopping sites. Providing random announcements for sales and keeping customers refreshing pages looking for the latest sales.

9. *Netflix "Postplay"*—A new feature on Netflix that automatically loads the next episode of a serial production. The introduction of this feature has led to bingeing on TV watching. (The same feature can be found on YouTube—how many toy videos do your kids watch?)

10. *Social interaction*—Adding social interaction to online posting sites attracts far more interest and far more users. Hipstamatic, a digital photography app for the iPhone, was eclipsed by Instagram, which offered the same core features but allowed users to post their photos on a social network tied to the app.

11. *Adrenal arousal*—Gaming companies employ
    neurobiologists and neuroscientists to engineer an
    addictive experience. They target blood pressure numbers
    of 180 over 120 within a few minutes of playing, combined
    with sweating (galvanic skin responses). If they do not
    achieve these goals, they tweak the game until the player
    elicits the proper response to the game.

I was raised in a Greek family, and we were a very emotive family—we hugged, we showed love, we made eye contact. Screen-raised children are prevented from developing resilience. They are profoundly fragile. We talk about psychological resilience. Parents need to be present with their kids. When the parent is distracted by their devices, this creates anxiety in the children. If the parent were out of the house, the child would just know that they would be back. It is unknown how this lack of development in socialization and manipulative skills will affect this generation in life and at work.

In our interview with Dr. David Greenfield, the founder of the Center for Internet and Technology Addiction and assistant clinical professor of psychiatry at the University of Connecticut School of Medicine, was asked about the effects of technology on this generation. Dr. Greenfield said:

> Well, we don't know what the long-term effects are yet because we haven't really had a full generation to grow up with that behavior…I think neurologically we suspect that there are going to be some changes in the neurochemistry or neurobiology, the way the brain operates, most of which probably will reverse if given the opportunity, although we don't know that for sure yet, because we haven't really done those longitudinal studies yet to look at what the end result

is. But again, you don't have to be a doctor to understand that if you raise a kid with a digital nanny, if you raise a kid with a screen, you're not giving them the nutritive value of social interaction. You can't provide nutritional social connection with a screen. And if you teach a kid to medicate themselves with the distraction that the screen provides, then they're unable to provide self-soothing. Yes, they're unable to soothe themselves internally. They rely on that external screen. They lack the capacity to modulate their own inner experience. That's dangerous, and we ran across that in our clinic all the time. The only way they know how to medicate themselves and make themselves feel better is to go online.[9]

Dr. Greenfield stated that these devices rely on text, graphics, and symbolic communication, which will not translate into real-time people skills that are necessary for one-on-one physical communication. The subtle nuances of interpersonal connection and intimacy aren't really translatable through symbolic gestures and emoticons and emojis. There is no way you can substitute real-time communication for communication through a smartphone via text, Snapchat, Messenger, or any of the other methodologies. These are tools that communicate certain facts and figures, but that does not work in terms of communicating the nuances of how we connect on a more intimate level. And I would contend that not only do they *not* communicate it, but they also block that communication because they are so distracting and time consuming and are so symbolic of creating a boundary around people's availability and accessibility for real-time connection. It does not facilitate real-time connection. Just walk into a waiting room or a line anywhere, and everybody's got their face on their screens. That does not communicate a willingness or a desire to connect on a human level.[10]

Another troubling topic is in the area of brain development. The human brain is not a finished organ at birth. An additional ten or twelve years are needed before even a general development is completed. When we think of the brain, we generally think about gray matter. White matter or myelin, on the other hand, is cable-like insulation covering the stemlike parts of neurons, called axons. Large groups of myelinated axons, which connect various regions in the brain, appear visibly as white matter. Myelination is an important part of normal brain development. The peak of myelination occurs during the first year of life but continues into young adulthood, especially in some cortical areas of the brain.[11] As we grow and learn, myelination increases in the area of the brain that needs it. There is evidence that myelin is affected by experience both during development and in adult life.[12] It appears that the extent of myelin sheath formation may adapt brain function to environmental stimuli. In other words, if you expose a child to repeated reading, the brain will respond by building myelin high-speed pathways that will serve the child for life.

Dr. Greenfield says that you can reform neural pathways:

> The brain has an amazing capacity for equal potentiality for neuroplasticity, so other areas of the brain can develop and you can build neural connections because the way it works is neurons that fire together, wire together. So the answer is, yes, you can get better and you can retrain the neural pathways of the brain. However, you've got to stop that negative behavior before you can do that. So in other words, you can't use screens all day and every day, all the time, and not have it impact your functioning. And so you're going to have to change your screen-based behavior in order to improve your functioning overall. So the answer is yes, but if you don't change your pattern of use, it'll probably regress back

to where it was. So a detox alone will not do it. It's got to change your path completely. And that's true, by the way, if you're watching your weight, you can lose weight. But if you don't change your overall patterns in relation to food, you're going to gain that weight back.[13]

According to Dr. Doreen Dodgen-Magee, psychologist and author of *Deviced!*:

It does appear that the most reliable research shows that four months of ten minutes a day mindfulness meditation doubles the gray matter in the region, the frontal prefrontal cortex and the cingulate, the cerebral cingulate. I think that study was more like six months of ten minutes a day. So changes in the path—and we know I'm definitely not an expert in neuroplasticity or neuropsychology—but we know that new neural pathways can be created all the way up to age 80. So what I love, what I can do to hear from folks is that the gray matter is the engine of the brain. The myelin sheaths are the efficiency.[14]

There is a correlation between myelination and various brain disorders. There are a plethora of studies that point to abnormalities in myelination driving various disorders, including attention deficit hyperactivity disorder (ADHD), autism in infants and children, schizophrenia, drug addiction in teens and young adults, and Alzheimer's in seniors. This volume of research has shown stunted myelination growth is correlated with drug addiction.

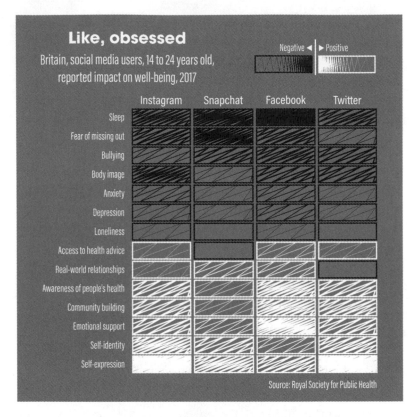

**Figure 21: Links between heavy use
of social media and mental illness**
(Royal Society for Public Health via *The Economist*)[15]

Technology's Impact on Students

A 2017 study published in the journal *Psicologia Educativa* investigating different aspects of technology used in the classroom and its effects on academic performance came up with mixed results.[16] The study analyzed factors such as:

- Technology use inside and outside of the classroom

- Multitasking in the classroom while studying

- Technological anxiety (FOMO)

- Executive functioning—includes cognitive processes that control attention and problem-solving as related to the choice to use or not use technology.

The researchers collected twenty-one days of smartphone usage from 216 students, resulting in:

- Students with higher levels of daily technology use had poorer academic performance.

- Students who showed a preference for multitasking and those who multitasked more while studying showed reduced academic performance.

- Higher levels of FOMO did not lead to lower academic performance.

- Higher levels of executive functioning were related to increased technology use and multitasking.

Interestingly, the cell phone tracking software measured the number of minutes each phone was unlocked, signifying use. The typical college student unlocked their phone sixty times per day for three to four minutes per unlock, which totaled 3.5 hours of usage per day.

The Science of Tech Addiction

The concern over cell phone addiction has encouraged French lawmakers to enact a ban on cell phone usage by students aged three to fifteen anywhere on school grounds. This law is a sweeping attempt to address the growing concern among parents and educators that this generation of children will grow up addicted to their mobile devices. Jean-Michel Blanquer, France's education minister, says the ban is intended to remove distractions during class and to encourage children to read a book or play outside during recreation.[17] He hopes the law will serve as a symbolic message to both children and adults beyond the school. How this ban will play out in real life is uncertain.

There is awareness, however, of the perils of the overconsumption of social media by the Gen Z cohort. Our national survey of Gen Zers found that 73% take their cell phone to bed while they sleep, and 85% check their social media just before bed and before getting out of bed in the morning.[18] The survey also found that 81% of Gen Zers have gone on a social media fast lasting one day to one month.

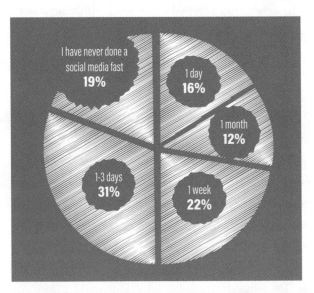

Figure 22: Gen Zer responses to whether they have ever gone on a social media fast (Nishizaki/DellaNeve)[19]

There is evidence that a ban can improve academic performance. A study performed at the London School of Economics found that standardized test scores rose the equivalent of an extra hour of school-work per week. The study measured sixteen-year-olds at ninety-one UK institutions between 2001 and 2011. Louis-Philippe Beland (economics, Carleton University), who led this study, believes that France's ban could help students.[20] Dr. Dodgen-Magee states that these technologies become obstacles to deeper learning: "Someone's going to have to do the hard thing of actually introducing and requiring some slower movement, some opportunities for deep work. And what I find with Gen Z folks is that they're desperate for opportunities to learn how to be quiet and still. But nobody has invested any time teaching them how to meditate or even do deep work on a single task in most work environments."[21]

There are many other studies concerning FOMO that have tried to assess whether alarm bells need to be raised. One factor that is consistent across all of these studies is the sheer amount of time Gen Zers spend on these devices. High school seniors spend an average of 2.25 hours per day texting, approximately 2 hours per day on the internet, 2 hours per day watching television, 1.5 hours per day on electronic gaming, and 0.5 hours per day on video chat, according to a recent survey.[22]

The results of our nationwide survey of working Gen Zers showed that on a daily basis, 22% spent 4 hours or more per day on social media, 16% spent between 3 and 4 hours, and 38% spent between 2 and 3 hours.[23] Within the social media usage category, 35% of respondents used video streaming services multiple times per day, while 30% used such services only once per day; that means 65% of social media usage included video streaming services on a daily basis. On the other hand, 75% of respondents claimed to still use Facebook, though this cohort has been moving to other social media platforms.

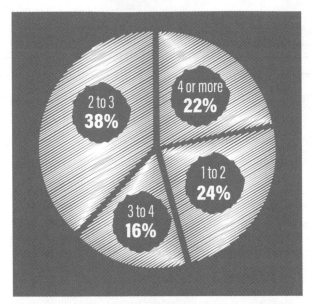

Figure 23: Gen Z hours per day on social media
(Nishizaki/DellaNeve)[24]

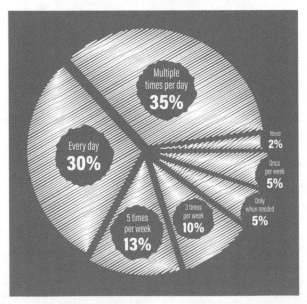

Figure 24: Gen Z video streaming and sharing usage
(Nishizaki/DellaNeve)[25]

Regarding technology fasting (or detox), Dr. Dodgen-Magee states, "So you spent a month without social media, without using technology? Everybody that's done it reports actually feeling happier. Once they start it, they feel uncomfortable at first; they feel ill at ease; they feel awkward. But within about three or four days, they actually report that they feel better, at least for the first time in a long time. Prior to this, they feel like they are on a digital treadmill, because they can't stop using it."[26]

Dr. Dodgen-Magee also says that research shows a relationship between video gaming and reduced resilience:

> Leonard Sax, the author of *Boys Adrift*, points out that video games do not engender resilience. How does that happen? How does excessive gaming lead to this lack of resilience? Well, there's something they're missing out on, or the way that I make sense of that is that most gaming platforms and most technology platforms exist on a fixed mindset model. Are you familiar with Carol Dweck's work? Yes. And that fixed mindset model which says you hit this to achieve whatever really is shown in the research. One hundred percent of the time, to make people top out of their potential early, do not expect as much of themselves to be less resilient, less grit. And so I think that's how I make sense of it, is that they are constantly in these environments where their prestige, their standing in the community is based on hitting these progressively more difficult fixed mindset models, and they're never being asked to take any kind of risks that involve the kind of personal fortitude that creates resilience.[27]

We are the most connected society in history. "Roughly seven-in-ten Americans say they ever use any kind of social media site—a share that has remained relatively stable over the past five years, according to a new Pew Research Center survey of U.S. adults" (see Figure 25).[28] YouTube and Facebook have captured the top three age categories of eighteen- to twenty-nine-year-olds, thirty- to forty-nine-year-olds, and fifty- to sixty-four-year-olds, respectively. Gen Zers spend far more time on Instagram, Snapchat, TikTok, and Twitter than other age cohorts.

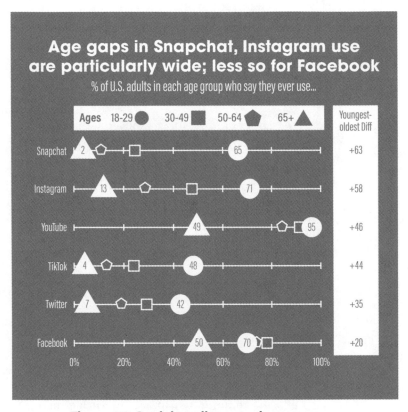

Figure 25: Social media usage by age group
(Pew Research Center)[29]

How do we know (or why do we suspect) that there may be an addiction problem with this behavior? It was recently reported that a juvenile had punched and knocked unconscious his sixty-three-year-old father outside of a restaurant in Yarmouth, Massachusetts. This occurred after his father had repeatedly asked him to stop texting. The juvenile was charged with assault and battery on a person over sixty with serious injury.

The military has seen increased issues with gaming addiction; in fact, infants have died as a result of physical abuse or neglect related to parents' constant gaming. The Department of Defense tracks child neglect related to gaming, identified as "electronic distractions." One of the telltale signs of gaming addiction was airmen with personal hygiene issues. DOD employees are given comprehensive training to recognize addictions and to identify who may be vulnerable.[30]

According to Dr. Greenfield, the World Health Organization included video game addiction in the *ICD-11* classification, the international classification of diseases, which is already out. He went on to explain:

> It's going to be adopted, I believe, this summer. So it is included. And therefore, theoretically, once those codes are in the billing systems, insurance companies should theoretically reimburse for it. If that's a treatment issue, of course, they should treat it. If it, in fact, is impacting the patient's daily functioning, which is the definition of a mental health or addiction issue. If it's impacting the ability to live and function in a normal way, then it absolutely needs to be included in insurance coverage. Is that going to happen next week or next month? I don't know. I mean, you've got to remember, insurance companies don't make their money by paying claims. So they're not going to be thrilled about this because it's yet another thing that they're going to have to pay. And I think they know that this is a huge problem and we're about to open a residential treatment program to treat this. And unless the insurance companies pay for it, people are going to

have to pay for it out of pocket initially. And it can be quite
expensive. So ultimately, if it's a real public health issue, then
insurance companies should cover it.[31]

These extreme forms of gaming addiction cannot and will not be
conflated with other milder forms of addiction to social media and
electronic devices. However, the widespread severity of addictions
can be categorized by using the American Psychiatry Association's
(APA's) *Diagnostic and Statistical Manual* (*DSM*), which categorizes
all psychiatric and behavioral disorders.

But what really causes addiction? How can one know if they are
susceptible to addictions? A child of alcoholic parents or drug-addict-
ed parents worries about whether they might suffer from the same
problems. Is this driven by genes or by the substances themselves?
All these substances impact dopamine in some fashion. Dr. Judson
Brewer, the director of research and innovation at the Mindfulness
Center and associate professor in behavioral and social sciences at the
School of Public Health and Psychiatry at the School of Medicine at
Brown University, agrees with this. He describes a process that starts
with a trigger. This could be a good or bad event, which is followed
by behavior and a reward. When this is repeated, it becomes a habit
or habit loop.[32]

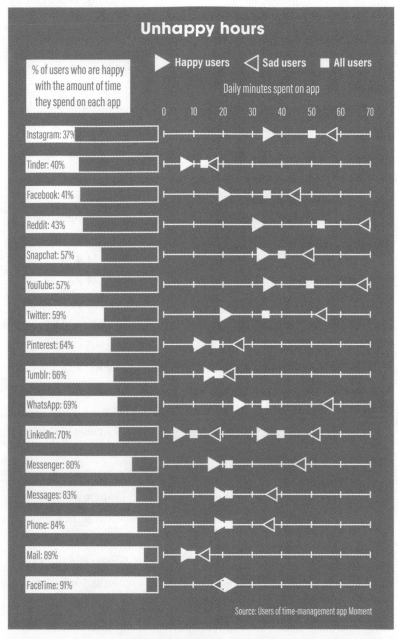

Figure 26: Percentage of users who are happy with time spent on social media (*The Economist*)[33]

Dopamine and serotonin are neurotransmitters, biochemicals that are manufactured in the brain. These biochemicals drive feelings and emotions and separate brain processes. These two biochemicals have separate brain pathways, regulatory schemes, and physiological and psychological outcomes. It's important to understand how these two chemicals work—specifically, how they work in concert or in opposition to each other. I will tie this into how and why this is important to our Gen Z cohort and why the potential effects are important to Gen Zers and to employers and educators.

In order for serotonin and dopamine to carry out their mission, they need the help of things called transport mechanisms. These behave like taxicabs ferrying passengers. The passengers of dopamine are the building blocks/amino acids of phenylalanine and tyrosine. The passenger of serotonin is tryptophan, which is found in eggs, poultry, and fish. The problem with these taxicabs is that the same cabs are required to transport serotonin and dopamine. The greater the frequency of reward-seeking behavior, the more often one is hailing a cab for dopamine. The poor passenger tryptophan is standing on the curb, waiting for an available cab on a cold, rainy night. In other words, frequent use of dopamine will consume the transport mechanisms for serotonin. No serotonin, no experience of contentment.

While these neurotransmitters compete for transport mechanisms, they are very different in terms of regulation. Dopamine receptors (think of receptors as the receiving side of a chemical signal or transaction) are susceptible to something called downregulation. Downregulation is more commonly called tolerance. When the receptor is continuously stimulated by the presence of dopamine, it can fail to respond to the dopamine, and if this continues, the receptor will eventually die. We see the effects of this in drug addiction. As receptors die off, the addict no longer experiences the effects of the drugs and needs to increase the dosage to achieve the same effects. Unfortunately, as the receptor die-off increases, dosage increases, and a lethal spiral ensues. The primary point here is that constant exercise of dopamine-inducing behaviors may lead to tolerance, which can lead to increased dopamine behaviors, which by definition may constitute addiction.

The interaction and competition between these chemicals are critical. There are multiple factors that can lead to increased reliance on dopamine: technology, processed food, sugar, decreased sleep, and drugs. These can lead to something called metabolic syndrome, which is associated with cardiovascular disease, cancers, obesity and hypertension, diabetes and Alzheimer's, and general chronic disease. (For more on this, see Gary Taubes's *Why We Get Fat: And What to Do About It*, Dr. Robert Lustig's *Fat Chance: Beating the Odds Against Sugar, Processed Food, Obesity, and Disease*, Dr. Jason Fung's *The Obesity Code*, and Nina Teicholz's *The Big Fat Surprise: Why Butter, Meat, and Cheese Belong in a Healthy Diet*, for a start.) The combination of stress and downregulation of dopamine will crowd out serotonin.

In our interview, Dr. Greenfield listed a few mediating activities:

> Meditation actually is a great antidote to high-tech living. And exercise also increases dopamine, which is the neuro-chemical, and if you're not going to be getting your hits of dopamine from screen use, you have better get it somewhere. And exercise is a wonderful way to do it. Other ways of doing it are eating and sex and other natural activities that give you pleasure. But if you rely on your main source of pleasure to be on a screen, you're going to have a pretty flat existence, and you're going to experience what we call reward deficiency syndrome, which is that you need a certain amount of screen stimulation to achieve pleasure. And if you don't get that screen stimulation, then you can't experience pleasure in any

other naturalistic part of your life. So when you go outside and you look at a tree, it's actually better than looking at trees online. Recently, we had somebody who told me of a kid who was asked to come outside and look at the eclipse of the moon. The youth said that he can see it online. So they lost the ability to experience real-time living.[34]

There are many studies associating depression with the use of electronics and media. There is plenty of research to support a connection between the underlying biological mechanisms and what we are seeing among our Gen Zers, their reports of depression and anxiety and the connection to technology.

Dr. Greenfield explains that there is a strong correlation between technology usage, depression, and anxiety:

> Well, I could tell you some of the research seems to indicate that there is a rise of depression and anxiety that correlates perfectly with the ultra-adoption of the smartphone, particularly, but internet technology in general. But really, it tracks the use of the smartphone pretty perfectly. So, I mean, we can't know. A correlation doesn't necessarily mean causality. But when you look at the mental health data in the United States and you look at the adoption of this technology, it's pretty shocking how high the correlation is between increased levels of overall depression, including suicidal ideation and behavior, along with generalized anxiety and a feeling of disenfranchisement from their social structures. And you don't have to be a doctor to look at the fact that people feel more disconnected and more alienated than ever, in spite of the fact that we have more ways to theoretically connect than ever before. You tell me by your observations, and you don't even have to be an expert in this subject. Do people

seem more connected today than they've ever been? I would say the complete opposite. People seem less connected. They don't feel as connected. That's what the research shows. In spite of the fact that we have a million apps and social media platforms to connect with. Nobody feels connected, certainly not through those applications. And so that's why I call it antisocial media. It's actually the antithesis of social media. Or social connection.[35]

Dr. Dodgen-Magee concurs with Dr. Greenfield:

I just think we've all become habituated now to high levels of technology use that those of us who are thinking about it know are correlated with depression and anxiety. I am sure that you've read the study out of the University of Philadelphia that shows causation. It shows causation between social media use and depression and anxiety...it's the first study to show causation, not just correlation. And it's a really, really well-done study. But yes, I think we need meditation rooms rather than gaming rooms in corporations. I think we need to actually enforce sometimes getting outside—like, sensory awareness is beyond just fidget spinners. And if corporations could begin to value these things in some ways, even if it's small steps, like an "Eyes Get Outside" campaign, rewarding employees for doing some active practice or volunteer work. But again, we still celebrate productivity. And I think to this generation, that just looks like distraction, which then interprets into anxiety and depression.[36]

Today few doubt the relationship between time spent on social media and electronic devices and depression and anxiety. It is not hard to imagine that there is a trade-off between various intellectual pursuits, going on various adventures, and taking on challenges that improve one's experience, knowledge, and skills and logging thousands of hours staring at electronic devices. Economists would call this trade-off the "opportunity cost." Given multiple choices in terms of time, personal energy, activities, and intellectual investment, which choice would provide the maximum benefit for a person?

When thinking about these opportunity costs, one immediately goes to a famous study called the Stanford marshmallow experiment, in which researchers tested the role of attentional processes in the voluntary delay of gratification of rewards. In this experiment, children were offered an immediate reward but were offered the choice of a greater reward if they waited. Two experiments were in place: in the first study, pretzels or animal cookies were used as the reward mechanisms, and in the second and more famous study, marshmallows were used as rewards.[37]

The children involved in these studies were followed up on in two additional studies, one produced in 1988 and the second in 1990. The 1988 study investigated the results of the delay in gratification on parents' competence ratings of their children. The competence ratings included personality-relevant items such as:

- Is verbally fluent, can express ideas well in language

- Uses and responds to reason

- Is attentive and able to concentrate

- Tends to go to pieces under stress, becomes rattled and disorganized

- Appears to feel unworthy, thinks of themself as bad

The study showed a relationship between the previous study's delay times and rated academic, social, and coping competence in adolescence. According to the parental ratings, those who delayed gratification longer were:

- more verbally fluent; used and responded to reason

- attentive and able to concentrate

- planful and thought ahead

- competent and skillful

- resourceful in initiating activities

- self-reliant and confident

- strongly involved in what they did

- could be trusted and were dependable

- self-assertive

- curious, exploring, and eager to learn

- concerned about moral issues

Beyond the anxiety and depression that have been quantified through many studies, it is impossible to predict what the effect of technology and technology addiction will be on the development of Gen Z. My conversations with Gen Zers have mirrored many studies in terms of the Gen Zers' awareness of tech addiction; this self-aware-ness has led many to go on technology fasts. It will be interesting to see the results of these opportunity costs. Those determined to master difficult skills or complex topics will need to sacrifice time and engage in prolonged attention and practice, which will require forgoing the pleasure of dopamine from technology. Who will be the medical doctors, scientists, engineers, Olympic athletes, dancers, artisans, and inventors of tomorrow? It's likely that success will be highly correlated to time spent away from the nonproductive use of technology.

WHAT CAN WE DO?

Why so much focus on technology, social media, internet addiction, and electronic device usage in a book about Gen Zers at work? Are we saying that electronic devices are bad and that everyone will be addicted and impaired? Are we saying that the sky is falling, or are we making generational comparisons to imply that previous generations were better in some form or fashion? The answer is no. We can compare technology addiction to alcohol usage. To some, pairing fine wine with food can be a beautiful dining experience. Six billion gallons of wine are consumed[38] each year in a mostly responsible way, but those with alcohol addictions have to avoid consumption or tread very carefully.

For most, technology usage is likely not going to lead to addictions. However, for those addicted, it (by definition) will disrupt and impair important learning and development. This has a direct impact on future employment and life in general, whether on the Gen Zer concerned with their readiness for the future, a parent, or a potential employer trying to grapple with future employee candidates; there needs to be awareness about the potential impacts of technology usage. Our national survey found that 47% of respondents thought that social media supported better relationships, while 34% felt that it had no impact and only 19% felt that it made relationships worse.[39] (This data is self-reported, and it would be quite interesting to survey their parents and employers.)

Since technology addiction may affect the majority of the Gen Z cohort, the time spent using technology is a critical factor in their lives. The economic term *opportunity cost* refers to a benefit that a person could have received but gave up to pursue another course of action. This cost is, therefore, most relevant for two mutually exclusive events. What occupies your time is a decision between mutually exclusive events. You can learn a language, eat a meal with a friend, go for a walk on a trail, or volunteer to help the poor—or you can surf the web, text friends, or watch videos on an electronic device.

The underdevelopment of socialization skills can greatly impact success at work. Author and science journalist Daniel Goleman's work on emotional intelligence (EI) lists five elements that comprise EI, which should be developed when one is younger (kindergarten through college); relatedly, it should not be entirely on the employer to help each employee become more emotionally intelligent (but to be realistic, corporations are going to have to help support their employees in a big way).[40] A global study conducted by researchers from the University of British Columbia, the University of Illinois, and the University of Chicago examined eighty-two different social-emotional learning programs involving more than ninety-seven thousand students from kindergarten to middle school yielded the following results: "Students who participated in programs graduated from college at a rate 11% higher than peers who did not. Their high school graduation rate was 6% higher. Drug use and behavior problems were 6% lower for program participants, arrest rates 19% lower, and diagnoses of mental health disorders 13.5% lower."[41]

As we already know, the APA ranked Gen Z as the generation most likely to report poor mental health.[42] Now that we have scared you about your kids' and your future employees' (and possibly your own) relationships with technology and social media, we thought it might be prudent to provide you with some data from experts in their fields who are working hard to combat FOMO, anxiety, depression, and other phenomena to help people live happier lives. All of this is important because it impacts you at home and at work, whether you're aware or not.

Mindfulness

Over the past couple of years, mindfulness has gained a lot of traction with Millennials and has become a buzzword in self-help and mainstream HR practices, but what does it mean? Mindful.org defines mindfulness as "the basic human ability to be fully present, aware of where we are and what we're doing, and not overly reactive or overwhelmed by what's going on around us,"[43] and this is counterintuitive in terms of what smartphones and social media have molded us to become—overly reactive to our "buzzes" and "beeps." Types of mindfulness include "being seated, walking, standing, and moving meditation, short pauses we insert into everyday life, and merging meditation practice with other activities such as yoga or sports."[44]

Dr. Dodgen-Magee has been successful with meditation techniques. During our interview, she discussed her visits to universities to teach this practice:

> And then they'd come up to me afterward and say, yeah, I don't know how to do it for ten minutes. So now every little talk I have with those age groups, I literally end with a ten-minute silence set. Then I have a little formula to teach them techniques, such as how to get into a posture to do that. Here's how we're going to breathe. Here's what we're going to do with distractions. They literally can't get enough of it. If I'm on a university campus, usually the administration will tell me, don't tell them you're going to do that because no one will come. I told them from my very first talk and there were two hundred people. Then my most recent had a thousand because they're hungry for it.[45]

A simple addition to your day and routine can generate tremendous results.

Exercise

I start work between 4:30 a.m. and 5:30 a.m. most days. This is because I have young children at home, and this is the only time I can fit a workout, which I consider the most important part of my workday, into my schedule. Exercising has always made me feel less stressed and given my mind a chance to wander and solve problems, when I'm not streaming movies or shows on my phone. So what's the science behind exercise? Can it help this generation (or any of us)?

Exercise has been shown to play a role in protecting against heart disease and diabetes, improving sleep, and lowering blood pressure. According to the Mayo Clinic, "regular exercise may help ease depression and anxiety by: releasing feel-good endorphins" and "taking your mind off worries"; it can help you "gain confidence…get more social interaction" (postpandemic), and "cope in a healthy way."[46] The Mayo Clinic also advises you to "check with your doctor before starting a new exercise program to make sure it's safe for you. Talk to your doctor to find out which activities, how much exercise, and what intensity level is OK for you. Your doctor will consider any medications you take and your health conditions. He or she may also have helpful advice about getting started and staying motivated."

Here are some additional exercise tips:

- The best exercise routine is the one that you will do regularly. I have a rule. Don't exercise for more than an hour. Find a routine that you can ideally get done in twenty minutes. Here's a tip (consult with your physician first): exercise to failure. If you are doing push-ups, do them slowly; your muscles will get tired more quickly. Do each set until you cannot push any longer. Only do one or two muscle groups, and switch out to a different set of muscle groups the next day. The evidence that you worked

to failure is a bit of soreness. See Dr. Ben Bocchicchio's
work for more on this concept. He's seventy-three years
old, by the way. Dr. Ted Naiman and William Shewfelt (of
Power Rangers fame) have a book called *The P:E Diet* and
cover this exercise concept in their book.

- Don't set overaggressive goals. If you are just starting out,
  use a routine for beginners. I wanted to learn how to do
  pull-ups. These are hard to do. I used a thick rubber band
  around the bar and would step on it to reduce the effort
  required. I did this for a year and eventually was able to
  do pull-ups without the rubber band. Now, I can do one
  hundred pull-ups in sets of ten to fifteen. It took years to
  get to this point. If you are struggling with push-ups, do
  them with your knees on the ground. If you are going for
  walks, start with a relaxed pace and shorter distances.

- Keep reading, watching YouTube videos, and
  experimenting with what works best for you. Don't
  compare yourself to some Special Forces person or
  marathon runner. If you don't feel that your routine is
  working well enough, find another routine, or make
  changes to obtain the best results in the shortest amount of
  time. Most people waste a lot of time in the gym. You don't
  have to spend a lot of time in the gym to get results.

Diet

According to the New Hampshire Department of Health and Human
Services, "Two hundred years ago, the average American ate only 2
pounds of sugar a year. In 1970, we ate 123 pounds of sugar per year.
Today, the average American consumes almost 152 pounds of sugar
in one year. This is equal to 3 pounds (or 6 cups) of sugar consumed

in one week!"[47] This alarming consumption of sugar has been identified through many studies. Just search for "sugar consumption and
depression," and you will find a plethora of research studies describing
the relationship between sugar consumption and depression.

I've been actively studying and experimenting with various eating patterns. It can be a religious war among favored-eating-pattern
devotees. Some examples are Whole30, Mediterranean, keto, paleo,
vegetarian, low carbohydrate healthy fat, low fat high protein, and
many more. Here is what I've learned:

- Processed foods, which were introduced in the 1970s,
  have caused the metabolic syndrome, diabetes, and obesity
  epidemics that we are living amid today.

- The various popular eating patterns seem to have similar
  characteristics:

  › The absence of processed foods. That's almost anything
    in a bag and in a box and includes industrial oils made
    from the seeds of plants such as corn, soybean, cotton,
    sunflower, and safflower. Sorry to say, but bread is
    processed food.

  › Most of these eating patterns recommend using fruit
    oils like olive and avocado oils, as well as (if you aren't a
    vegetarian) animal-based fats like butter, lard, and tallow.

  › The primary ingredients in most popular eating
    patterns are fish, meat, eggs, poultry, and fresh
    cruciferous vegetables—these are the less-starchy, lower-
    carbohydrate vegetables such as broccoli, cauliflower,
    brussels sprouts, cabbage, etcetera. Basically, above-
    ground-grown and usually green vegetables.

Personal Connection

Now that we've discussed ways to help you feel better about yourself in order to increase your physical and mental health, let's add another component: people.

Below are the components of Daniel Goleman's emotional intelligence model and descriptions of how we can use it to get along better with people.[48]

1. *Self-Awareness*: Knowing what we are feeling at the moment and using those preferences to guide our decision-making; having a realistic assessment of our own abilities and a well-grounded sense of self-confidence.

    How can Gen Z (or even a lot of adults) have self-awareness if we block people who don't agree with us on social media? How can we become equipped with the right tools to help? Goleman states that self-awareness includes emotional self-awareness, "the ability to read and understand your emotions as well as recognize their impact on work performance, relationships, and the like," an accurate self-assessment, and self-confidence: "A strong and positive sense of self-worth."

    One of the great tools that I use in my training to help with teams and leaders in the workplace is the CliftonStrengths Assessment. This personality assessment is backed by scientific data that shows what's *right* with us but also gives folks a chance to see where they might have blind spots or even basements, which is how *other* people see us. I have been using this assessment for my college undergraduate soft-skills courses, and the students love it. (I didn't take my first personality test until my doctorate program, which reflects a lacking in our educational system in terms of self-awareness.) This tool helps accomplish all three components of Goleman's self-awareness, so the college students can use it to manage their strengths and weaknesses without taking it personally (it's pretty hard to block an assessment, right?), understand when their natural talents have a positive or negative impact at work (and in their personal lives), and help build confidence by utilizing personal strengths.

2. *Motivation*: Using our deepest preferences to move and guide us toward our goals.

3. *Self-Regulation*: Handling our emotions so that they facilitate rather than interfere with the task at hand; being conscientious and delaying gratification to pursue goals; recovering well from emotional distress.

4. *Empathy*: Sensing what people are feeling, being able to take on their perspective, and cultivating rapport and attunement with a broad diversity of people. Considering other people's feelings, especially when making decisions.

    Think about the time when you read (or wrote) a snarky email. Did you have a chance to see that person in a meeting or talk to them on the phone? I've noticed in my career that once people see you or hear your voice, it's hard for them to be a jerk because they have empathy and may be averse to conflict. Social media has taken these types of interactions away, as you "like" a post that might be seen as rude or hurtful or even write negative comments about someone's physical features. I doubt one would be so bold as to say the same thing to another's face or on the phone. Also, as discussed earlier in this chapter, there is evidence to suggest that when oxytocin is released, empathy can be enhanced.[49]

5. *Social Skills*: Handling emotions in relationships well and accurately reading social situations and networks; interacting smoothly; using these skills to persuade and lead, negotiate and settle disputes, for cooperation and teamwork.

Goleman's primary thesis is that the intelligence quotient (IQ) is important for "getting in the door" but that EI is important for success in the workplace.

Here is some advice from Dr. Greenfield: "Learn. Take a course in civics, take a course in human communications or in human relations. Do some learning in the arts, do things that are real, time-based, not screen-based. Even though you can look at some pictures of a place you want to visit, go visit it instead. In other words, don't do everything online. That would be my advice."[50]

CONCLUSION

As you can see, technology plays an important role in our lives. It helps us to stay in touch with our loved ones, send an email from anywhere in the world, and even teach kids virtually during a pandemic. But as with all things, there must be balance and moderation. We've conveyed information from some of the top smartphone addiction experts in the world about the negative effects of technology and how we can fight back to ensure that we're in control so that it's not in control of us. The next section of the book will focus exclusively on how to recruit, retain, work with, and lead Gen Z.

EXERCISES

1. How much time do you spend on social media per week? Do you think this impacts your productivity?

2. Do you feel happier when you decrease screen time? If you have kids (or grandkids), does increasing or decreasing screen time have an impact on them? What does this impact look like?

3. What do you think are the long-term effects of increased screen time for you and your family?

4. How do FOMO and technology affect your workplace? Have you noticed a difference in interpersonal skills among younger employees?

5. Do you think FOMO and technology addiction are short-term or long-term problems? Why or why not?

   Please list the ways in which you can help solve this challenge based on what you have read so far:

Part 2

RECRUITING, RETAINING, AND REIMAGINING THE FUTURE WORKFORCE

FOUR
RECRUITING AND RETAINING GEN Z

INTRODUCTION

Imagine that you are the hiring manager for your company and you have spent hours of time putting together a job description for a position that is desperately needed by your team. Once the job description has been completed and you get the buy-in from senior executives to approve the new position, you call your recruiter, who goes on to spend hours reviewing resumes, interviewing candidates, and whittling down the top three candidates for you, your boss, and senior management to interview. Once these interviews are complete, you select your top candidate, extend the offer, and are excited about adding this person to your team. A couple of days go by, and you do not hear from your top candidate. Your recruiter continues to call, email, and text them but receives no response. In what seems like a bad dating dream, *you've been ghosted*! How could this have happened? What did you do wrong? Could you have offered more money? "Just give me another chance!" you say, but all you hear is crickets.

This story we just told is semifictional, but such scenarios are becoming more and more common in the recruiting world. Gen Zers are starting to ghost recruiters or not show up for their first day of work without any explanation—*companies* are being ghosted. For those of you who do not know what being "ghosted" means, it is when someone cuts off all contact with you without an explanation.

RECRUITMENT AND RETENTION ROI

A great deal of effort goes into recruiting and retaining America's finest employees to give organizations a competitive advantage, but what happens when these new recruits quit their job after six months? Two years? Or aren't even interested? According to Gallup's "State of the American Workplace" report, 35% of employees have changed jobs within the past three years, and 91% of employees left their company in the process (i.e., *voluntarily*).[1] Our study found that 51% of Gen Zers plan to move to three to five different companies in their career, followed by zero to two (29%) and six to eight (16%). As the economy improves, employees will have more options and will not settle to work for a company that does not align with their values.

There are tremendous costs associated with recruiting, training, and retaining the workforce. Since both authors are data-driven people, we're going to throw a lot of numbers at you in the next two paragraphs to show you the financial impact of the importance of recruiting and retaining top talent, and we'll do our best to simplify it for you. According to a 2016 "National Study of Employers" report by the Society for Human Resource Management (SHRM), the average cost per hire is $4,129, and the time it takes to fill a position is forty-two days. (Keep in mind that Gen Zers' attention span is less than that of a goldfish!)[2] In conjunction with the cost of recruitment (money and time), the Center for American Progress reports that the typical cost of turnover is approximately 21% of an employee's annual salary and, for C-level jobs, can tend to be up to 213% of annual salary.[3] In addition, the average turnover rate for an employee is 19% (12% for voluntary, 6% for involuntary).[4] Do we have your attention?

Here's a simplified hypothetical: You own a small company of one hundred employees with an average annual salary of $40,000, with a turnover rate of 19% at a turnover cost of 21% (of $40,000), and you can take a $159,600 hit ([.21 x 40,000] x 19 = $159,600). So, what can we do to help you alleviate this? Glad you asked! The next sections of this chapter will provide ways to help your organization recruit and retain this new generation, as well as help to improve the lives of the existing generations you already employ—gotta keep those Gen Zers happy!

This chapter is going to discuss different topics that relate to recruiting and retaining Gen Z based on our own research, as well as secondary sources. But before we go there, it's important to break down the difference between recruiting and retaining employees. If you already know this, please feel free to skip to the next section.

THE FOUR *P*s OF RECRUITMENT—GETTING THEM TO ACCEPT YOUR FRIEND REQUEST

As I was writing this section, I noticed the similarities between HR recruiting and the marketing mix framework. For those of you who don't know what a marketing mix is, I'll give you a quick overview. The marketing mix consists of the **Four *P*s of Marketing: product (or service), place, price, and promotion (how you communicate your message).** In the middle of your marketing mix, you have the target market (specific customer) you are trying to sell to, which may include demographics, psychographics, and geographics. In the case of recruitment, your target market is the Gen Zer you want to hire and may consist of the following demographics: new college graduate with a specific concentration, GPA, campus involvement, internship/work experience, letters of recommendation, etcetera; the psychographics will be hard to discern from a resume, but you make sure the Gen Zer you hire will be a good fit within the culture (start-up, government,

Fortune 50 company, nonprofit, etc.), which can be discussed during the interview process. Check out the chart below for an illustration, and see the blank chart on our website or at the end of this chapter to help get you started.

Target Market Checklist

Who are you trying to recruit for your organization, based on your job description?

- College grad? If so, how many years out?

- Internship experience? If so, what type of firms?

- Professional experience (outside of internships)?

- What college majors do you prefer? GPA requirements? Club/leadership positions on campus?

- Are you trying to get more diversity in your organization, and are you recruiting from diverse colleges and providing equitable opportunities for all potential candidates?

- Certifications (Microsoft Office, Tableau, etc.)?

- Geographic location? Are you willing to pay them to relocate?

Product—Job Description, Corporate Culture, Core Values

The job: As in the marketing mix, we must first start with what you're trying to sell the Gen Zers: your company, core values, culture, and the job itself. Before you start your target market checklist, you need to write the job description. Is the job description relevant to the *actual* tasks your future Gen Zer will perform? Is it unreasonable?

I remember that when I graduated from college in 2007, a lot of the entry-level jobs that were posted online required a degree with three to five years of experience, which was preposterous. If I had three to five years of experience in that field, why would I apply for an entry-level position? I know I sound like a venting Millennial, but this type of unfair environment drove me to go get an MBA to make me a more competitive candidate. (Side fact: I worked full-time in sales for three years while going to school full-time and still didn't get callbacks. Recessions suck, but so do pandemics; we feel for you, Gen Z!)

Company: What does your company actually do to keep the lights on? If you make construction hardware, what type of projects can you highlight to employees that you take pride in? What type of impact does your organization have in your community, the environment, and the world? What are your thoughts and actions on social justice?

Culture: What are your core values? How are these reflected in the day-to-day operations of your organization?

Environmental Concerns

Interesting story: So back in the summer of 2020, I was asked to do a presentation for an HR professional association about the impact of the COVID-19 pandemic on the multigenerational workplace, and while doing research, I found Deloitte's "Global Millennial Survey 2020," which stated that the top concern Gen Z had *during* the pandemic was climate change and protecting the environment, while Millennials' top concern was health care/disease prevention.[5] This survey was conducted between April 28, 2020, and May 17, 2020, during the first wave of the pandemic and shutdowns, and Gen Z was *more* concerned about the environment than health care/disease prevention. When I read the results of this survey, I was completely shocked (in a good way) by Gen Z's commitment to and concern for the environment.

Interestingly enough, studies of the 2020 election "based on votes counted as of November 18, suggest that 52%–55% of voting-eligible young people, ages 18–29, cast a ballot in the 2020 presidential election. Using the same methodology and data from a week after the election in 2016, we had previously estimated that youth voter turnout in 2016 was 42–44%."[6] The Center for Information & Research on Civic Learning and Engagement (CIRCLE) data indicates 61% of youth (ages eighteen to twenty-nine) voted for Joe Biden, and 36% voted for President Trump.

Would this have anything to do with Trump pulling out of the Paris Agreement on climate change and threatening to cancel the Gen Z social media app TikTok? Maybe, maybe not, but it was interesting to see a record turnout of Gen Zers/young Millennials for Biden over Trump. CIRCLE found that 52% of young voters were "very concerned" about climate change, and 49% of young voters "strongly opposed" building a wall at the border to limit immigrants, compared to 33% of voters of all ages.

Work Schedule

We wrote a good portion of this book prepandemic, and it's kind of ironic to look back at this section and see how most folks have been *forced* to trust and allow their employees to telecommute and work on their own schedule (most of the time).

As stated earlier, flexible hours are one of the major causes of generational friction because we have moved from time-based labor to task-based labor. The Society for Human Resource Management defines flextime as "allowing employees to change their arrival and departure times on a periodic basis" and flexplace as "allowing employees to work at home or offsite,"[7] while the Department of Labor's website defines a flexible work schedule as "an alternative to the traditional 9 to 5, forty-hour work week. It allows employees to vary their arrival and/or departure times. Under some policies, employees must work a prescribed number of hours a pay period and be present during a daily 'core time.'"[8] The same 2016 SHRM "National Study of Employers" report found that 81% of employers allow some employees to periodically change their quitting times, while 42% of employers allow some employees to change starting and quitting times on a daily basis.[9]

After leaving the corporate world (cubicles, break rooms, drawn-out meetings, and, yes, a *steady paycheck*) behind, I suddenly felt a big weight off my shoulders in having the ability to work from home or spend a peaceful afternoon at a Starbucks (to avoid traffic while waiting for a client meeting), working on my laptop while sipping a pumpkin spice latte. I have a friend who moved from DC to Kentucky to work 100% remotely and save money on living expenses.

So, when does Gen Z want to come into the office/log on to their work computer in their pj's? We found that 48% of Gen Zers in our study prefer to work a nine-to-five job, 24% prefer to work from 6:00 a.m. to 2:00 p.m., and only 11% prefer to work from 12:00 p.m. to

8:00 p.m., contrary to stereotypes about recent college grads wanting to roll into the office around noon.

Changing the work schedule to the rotating day off (RDO) or 4/10 schedule can also be advantageous to entice this generation. An RDO schedule usually consists of working nine days, with one day off, or four nine-hour days and one eight-hour day one week, then the next week four nine-hour days with that Friday off. The 4/10 schedule consists of working ten hours a day, four days a week, with *every* Friday off.[10] There can still be flexible starting and quitting times within the nine- or ten-hour days, but giving a twenty-two-year-old a three-day weekend every week or every other week would be a great selling point! When I graduated business school, I was on the RDO schedule and was able to take quick trips to visit my mom in Portland, explore New York, and do homework, which was very valuable to me and was one of the main reasons I stayed at that company as long as I did (besides the mission and great coworkers).

As you can see, Gen Z had an influence on the election (especially in those swing states), and if yours is an organization trying to recruit this generation, it's really important to know their values and how you can *authentically* cater to them to recruit top talent to your organization.

Price—Salary, Benefits, and Perks (Free Food?)

How competitive is your starting salary for the position? What are your company perks?

Compensation ("Adulting" Is Hard Work)

According to Gallup, "41% of employees say a significant increase in income is 'very important' to them when considering a new job," while Millennials and Gen Xers rate this as a higher priority during a job search than Baby Boomers.[11] This must have to do with the fact that Millennials and Gen Zers combined have the most people living in poverty.[12] In addition, the Pew Research Center found that Gen Z and Millennial men (eighteen- to thirty-four-year-olds) are more likely to live with a parent than to live with a spouse or partner, and "living with a parent is the most common young adult living arrangement for the first time on record."[13] Even though we're wrapping up this book during the pandemic, starting pay/raises may be volatile for the next year or two, but according to the National Association of Colleges and Employers (NACE), the average pay per year for college graduates from 2018 to 2019 increased from $50,944 to $53,889—a 5.8% increase.[14] We know that pay may vary depending on major or specialty, but this should help you gauge how close you are to the national average, and we recommend that you look up NACE's latest numbers to see how you compare.

If you have a college degree and took out student loans, then you'll probably remember the day you got a bill for your first student loan payment six months after you graduated. It's no wonder that Gen Z is getting side gigs (Uber, Lyft, freelance, etc.) to help pay off their student loans and survive in today's economy. Our Gen Z survey found when we asked, "If your primary job paid you more, would you quit your side job(s)?" 70% of respondents said they would indeed quit, and only 30% said they would continue working their side gig.

According to a study by NACE, 56.8% of employers forecast giving the graduating class of 2018 signing bonuses, compared to the 2016 bonus rate of 57.3%.[15]

Our study found that 59% of the Gen Zer respondents got a side gig during the pandemic (on top of their normal job), but 70% would quit their side gig if their company paid them more. Paying an employee more doesn't happen overnight and certainly is tough to do during a pandemic, but we have a solution for you: *Be OK with their side gig!*

(83% of the Gen Zers surveyed said that they would like their company to be accepting of their side jobs.) We know, this is a new world, and it is no longer taboo to have a job outside of your primary one, but ensure that they (Gen Zers and other workers) understand the clear guidelines for doing a satisfactory job in their primary job first and confirming their side gig is not a conflict of interest (such as working for a competitor or supplier/vendor, participating in illegal activities, etc.).

Tuition Reimbursement

One of the best perks I enjoyed when I entered the corporate environment was receiving tuition reimbursement. I couldn't believe it! *Wait, they're going to give me money for tuition? And with no strings attached?* (This is not common, but it is a sweet deal.) My mindset at the time was: that's money left on the table that I am not taking advantage of if I'm not developing myself. Realistically, most companies have policies that if the employee leaves within a year or two of receiving the tuition reimbursement, they have to pay it back. (Ouch!)

So why offer tuition reimbursement? One survey found that 79% of recipients found tuition reimbursement to be an important factor in considering working for their company (*recruitment*), and 81% said this perk made it more likely they would stay with the company (*retention*).[16]

According to a 2016 SHRM survey, 61% of employers offered some sort of tuition reimbursement, with the average being approximately $4,000 (which may or may not pay for your textbooks and backpacks).[17] In all seriousness, though, according to the College Board, the average cost for in-state registered full-time student tuition for 2021–2022 was $10,740.[18] If you fall into the average and your company pays $4,000 a year, that's a little less than half—still a great perk! Ironically enough, only 6% of employees take advantage of this opportunity.[19]

A 2015 study published by Georgetown University's Center on Education and the Workforce found that employers spend $1.1 trillion (yes, trillion) on formal and informal higher education and training.[20] Of that $1.1 trillion, colleges and universities spend $407 billion on formal education annually, while employers spend $177 billion.[21] Since 1994, colleges and universities have increased spending on formal education for their employees by 82%, compared to a 26% increase in such spending by employers.[22] This is a booming industry for a reason: employees want to continue to develop and better themselves, and companies have been the primary conduit to help make this happen, whether it be through vocational or personal development. Why does this matter? Our study found that over 70% of respondents would like their employer to provide tuition reimbursement, as well as student loan repayment, which means that the expectations are very high if employers want to recruit and retain top-talent Gen Zers.

As a college professor, I like to poll my undergraduate students on how many of them plan to attend graduate school. In having tuition reimbursement programs to support your employees, you're helping them level up, adding value to your company while they are working with you (leadership is usually a core class in MBA programs), and most importantly, you're showing that you are willing to invest in their professional development and future.

Tuition/Training ROI

As a manager or leader within your organization, you may or may not be asking, "What's my company's ROI for paying for my employee's MBA when they leave to pursue a higher-paying job?" Great question! Cigna performed a study that calculated the ROI of tuition reimbursement and found:

- For every $1 that Cigna invested in their Educational Reimbursement Program (ERP), they got back their $1 and avoided an additional $1.29 in talent management costs.

- "ERP participants achieve more promotions than non-participants (10% more likely to be promoted), resulting in lower cost to fill."

- "ERP participants achieve more internal transfers than non-participants (7.5% more likely to receive a transfer), resulting in a lower cost to fill."

- "ERP participants are retained more than non-participants (8% more likely to be retained), resulting in reduced turnover costs."[23]

If you need an additional incentive, turn to Uncle Sam. According to SHRM, "Section 127 of the Internal Revenue Code provides an exclusion of up to $5,250 per calendar year from an employee's gross income for amounts received by the employee, provided that certain requirements are met." (See the IRS code for more details.)[24]

Gallup found that "Millennials are more likely than both Gen Xers and Baby Boomers to say a job that accelerates their professional or career development is 'very important' to them (45% of Millennials vs. 31% of Gen Xers and 18% of Baby Boomers)."[25] Our study found that the majority of Gen Zers have strong preferences for learning a job outside of the job they were hired for, so tuition reimbursement and job rotation programs are great perks in recruiting efforts.

Student Loan Repayment (Say What?)

As I receive my monthly emails that my automatic payment on my student loan was just processed (yes, a doctorate from a top school is expensive), I dream of the day when this equivalent of a luxury car payment (or mortgage, depending on where you live) will go away. I am very grateful that I had the opportunity to be accepted into Pepperdine's top-ranked organizational leadership doctoral program and complete it in less than three years (yes, tuition is expensive—no time to waste on getting that ROI!), but student loan debt is a serious problem in this country, and some economists are saying that it will be the next bubble to pop.

Did you know that enrollments in income-based repayment plans more than tripled between 2014 and 2019?[26] A whopping 44.7 million Americans have student loan debt; this debt totals $1.47 trillion and is the second most significant form of debt after mortgages. (Yes, it surpassed credit card and auto loans!)[27] Even parents and grandparents are now taking out loans for their kids and grandkids.

With student debt soaring to record numbers, companies and their employees are starting to enter into a marriage-like agreement: *I come with student loan debts that I'd like you to pay!* That's right! Some employers (currently, only 4%[28]) are sensitive to the amount of debt that college graduates have accumulated and are offering to help pay for their employees' student loans or help them consolidate them by working with local financial institutions to obtain more favorable interest rates. Even Congress has taken action. The Consolidated Appropriations Act, passed at the end of 2020, extended the CARES Act student loan provisions to allow employers to make tax-exempt loan-repayment contributions of up to $5,250 through 2025.[29]

Even though tuition loan repayment is currently considered taxable income, empathetic companies will match student loan repayments for employees. Even if a company paid fifty dollars a month, I think that most young people would appreciate the effort and thoughtfulness and could allocate it toward their principal loan balance.

Question: How much can you allocate in your budget next year for tuition repayment? If you think this is a ridiculous question, what's your current cost of turnover?

Free Food and Other Perks

I remember working in the semipublic sector out of business school and having to pay for my own lunch at our holiday party, as well as bring my own water and coffee. When I worked in the private sector, we had beer Fridays, unlimited water and K-Cups, free cereal every day, and free bagel Mondays—the Millennial in me was very happy!

Free food is one of the coolest perks in an office, and among the Gen Zers we surveyed, "free food" led as the number one perk Gen Zers would like from their employer (38%), followed by a tie between exercise-related perks like gym membership and yoga (14%) and sit/stand desks (14%), then dual monitors (13%). It seems that corporations are getting wise to this, and as of 2018, 32% of employers offered snacks and beverages, compared to 20% in 2014.[30] Every corporate culture is different, but we think it's important to poll your workers to see what they would like to help make their experience more enjoyable.

Promotion—Website, Social, Texts, and More

If you're looking to recruit for an entry-level position from outside your company (most likely Gen Z), common recruitment strategies include targeting passive or active candidates, posting online, managing your employer brand and image (very important for Gen Z, as you'll see in the next section), managing the candidate experience (recruiters aren't the only ones doing the ghosting anymore), and measuring results.[31] Gen Zers really care about what their friends think of their experience at a company and will most likely take their friends' recommendations (83% according to our study) or take a position that sounds cool in their latest TikTok or Instagram feed.

I remember applying to a company in October following graduation from business school, going through multiple rounds of interviews with managers and senior-level executives, then receiving radio silence. The recruiter didn't ghost me, but I didn't hear anything for months. I really wanted to work for this company, so I held out and didn't apply to other companies. Luckily, the holdout worked, and I got an offer at the end of February—four months later! Gen Zers do not have the patience to wait weeks or months to hear back from the recruiter and could possibly ghost the recruiter when they finally get the offer because they may not want to deal with the conflict of telling them they took another position.

You can attract Gen Z employees by, to name a few strategies, hiring a third-party recruiter; using a temp firm; attending recruiting events at high schools, technical schools, colleges, and universities (are these diverse student populations?); utilizing government and community-based programs; utilizing public relations (PR); drawing from employee referrals; and taking advantage of boomerang employees.[32]

Some of the biggest questions you want to ask yourself when recruiting this next generation are: How authentic is your recruiting process? Do you have a website/social media accounts dedicated to recruiting college grads/Gen Zers? Are your recruiters knowledgeable about your brand? Do they represent diversity? What is their level of customer service and follow-up with potential candidates? Does your company have a corporate social responsibility (CSR) strategic plan? Does this CSR plan involve protecting the environment? Can your recruiters articulate this? All of these questions are extremely important to Gen Z and can impact your chances of recruiting them as potential employees for your company.

Place—Office, Remote, or Hybrid?

As of finalizing our book in March 2022, there is currently a divide between workers and organizations about where the future of work will take place. Will we be fully remote, adopt a hybrid workstyle (two to three days in person), or go back to fully in-person offices? In an effort to help employers, we included the issue of where work will take place for Gen Z in our national study.

Our prepandemic study found that over 80% of Gen Zers preferred to work at brick-and-mortar locations, as well as working remotely. Our national study during COVID-19 found that 50% of respondents would consider moving out of state if given the opportunity to work 100% remotely; another 31% said maybe. This is a great data point for Gen Z employers because you may be able to get the best talent with this recruitment hack, but you need to ensure that you have the right infrastructure/processes in place to enable you and your Gen Zers to be successful.

Gallup found that 43% of US workers work remotely in some capacity, a much lower percentage than the preference rate indicated by our study.[33] A 2016 SHRM and Families and Work Institute report found the percentage of employers allowing telecommuters increased from 33% in 2012 to 40% in 2016.[34] There are currently 3.9 million telecommuters who work from home at least half of the time.[35] With those 3.9 million workers who telecommute half-time or full-time, it is estimated that 7.8 billion miles are not being traveled, three million tons of greenhouse gas are avoided, and $980 million in gas savings is achieved.[36] (Tip: Remember, Gen Z is very keen on trying to help the environment. This could be a great selling point when trying to recruit this generation, and it could save some cash.)

In addition to saving the environment and time, full-time telecommuters save over $4,000 per year, while half-time remote employees still save, on average, $2,677 per year on commuting costs, food, tax breaks, and professional attire.

MIT's Sloan School of Management found that when flextime was introduced—working remotely two to three days a week, working in the office on Wednesdays, not working the nine-to-five hours explicitly but rather being mindful of other stakeholders' schedules and not having an expectation of being connected 24-7—it resulted in a 100% likelihood of recommendation of this program to other departments.[37]

Global Workforce Analytics found that employers can save over $11,000 per half-time telecommuter per year based on the following metrics: increased productivity creates a decrease of costs by 15%, real estate costs decrease by 25%, absenteeism decreases by 31%, and voluntary turnover decreases by 10%.[38]

Question: What's your telecommuting plan? Can it be revised to accommodate Gen Z? Our study found that Gen Zers prefer face-to-face communication over any other type of communication, so just offering this option may be enticing, even if it's not utilized to extremes.

According to an analysis of the US Census by Global Workforce Analytics, the five professions that telecommute the most are "Management (16% telecommute), Office and Administrative Support (14%), Sales and Related (13%), Business and Financial Operations (9%), and Computer and Mathematical (9%)."[39] We understand that there are a lot of industries in which you cannot telecommute, so those not interacting with customers daily might have the first opportunities. (Although doctors and other professionals are doing consultations via "telehealth" to help stop the spread of COVID-19.)

Prepandemic, Global Workforce Analytics found that "40% more US employers offered flexible workplace options in 2015 than in 2010, but still only 7% make it available to most of its people."[40] In addition, larger organizations with over five hundred people are most likely to make telecommuting available to most of their people (12%), compared to smaller companies with under one hundred people (5%). Ironically, only "3% of organizations with flexible and remote work programs conduct any sort of formalized analysis" to measure the effectiveness (or not) of telecommuting on their organization.[41]

If an employee telecommutes two days a week and has a one-hour round-trip commute each day, they can save one hundred hours per year (excluding two weeks for vacation). James and I currently live in Southern California, and if we have an 8:00 a.m. meeting somewhere, we both have to leave the house between 5:00 a.m. and 5:30 a.m. to beat the traffic. For those of you reading this book who live and work in less trafficked areas, congratulations, and I hope you enjoy your ten-minute drive to work (bitter tone)! Besides time savings, working remotely can help decrease stress.

AAA performed a national study that found that "more than 78% of drivers report having engaged in at least one aggressive driving behavior at least once in the past year"; the most common behaviors were "purposefully tailgating another vehicle, yelling at another driver, and honking their horn to show annoyance or anger."[42] After my one-to-two-hour commute each way, I feel tired and drained, and it takes me some time to bounce back.

In addition to decreasing stress from traffic, sometimes working from home can make you more productive. During my corporate tenure, a lot of my work was done face-to-face, but about once a month, I would work from home because it was almost impossible to get spreadsheets or other types of reports done without people bursting into my cubicle or office. In addition to constant interruptions, office gossip can be a distraction. Now, we're not going to be naive and say that if you work from home, you won't be sucked into the office gossip machine. (Heard of Instant Message [IM] or Slack? We'll cover that more in the "Working with Gen Z" chapter.) Removing yourself from a toxic or political environment can help increase your productivity, but with the advancement of technology, anything can be distracting.

It is also important to note that telecommuting *all* the time is not for everyone. According to Gallup's latest research, "Employees who work remotely 100% of the time are among the least engaged," as only 30% engaged in their work.[43] Also, we found from our survey that once the pandemic is over, 35% of the Gen Zers would like to work remotely 50% of the time, with 31% wanting to work remotely 25% of the time and 15% wanting to work 100% remotely.

When the pandemic hit, one of the big concerns was the potential for increased depression and anxiety among employees who were forced to work from home at a moment's notice. According to the Kaiser Family Foundation, a nonprofit organization providing information on national health issues, in July 2020, "the majority of adults (53%) 18 and older said that worry and stress related to coronavirus have had a negative impact on their mental health, up from 39% in May," and four in ten adults were reporting symptoms of anxiety or depression in July, and younger adults were more likely to experience depression or anxiety.[44] Our study found that 49% of Gen Zers admitted that working remotely has made their levels of anxiety and depression increase. In our survey, 56% of Gen Zers confessed to feeling lonely at times while working remotely.

James and I have been working from home for years, so we got used to not seeing our coworkers every day, but I remember when I first started my company; as an extreme extrovert, I really missed those watercooler and hallway conversations and was slightly lonely in the beginning but eventually adjusted and embraced getting tasks done quickly without interruption. But the difference between us *intentionally* working from home and the global pandemic was that in the latter scenario a large percentage of the workforce was *forced* into this new lifestyle and had to adapt their home and work lives into one big cluster of workday and *distance learning*.

We know that life will eventually go back to the "new normal" and some of the COVID-19 content of this book may not be completely relevant, but we'd like to use this opportunity to highlight some of the challenges that employees, employers, and parents had to face during the pandemic, as well as in light of working from home more generally.

PricewaterhouseCoopers (PwC) offers some great ways to stay connected to your team while working remotely:

- Daily group check-ins with your team; turn your camera on (we'll get to more of this later)

- Leaders have "office hours" in the mode of professorial office hours (maybe more people will show up there than do to mine!)

- Shared calendars and tracking tasks

- Virtual happy hours/coffees/lunch breaks

- Quick walk-and-talk as a team

- Virtual book clubs

- "Let people get to know your new 'coworkers' (spouses, children, roommates, and/or pets) by hosting an event where everyone can mingle virtually."[45]

RETENTION/TURNOVER—KEEPING THEM ENGAGED AND HAPPY

Now that we have talked about how to get Gen Zers to your organization, we're going to talk about how to keep them engaged and with your company as long as possible. (Do we have to go over the math again?) Please note that a lot of these tools can apply to any generation, and you can start implementing them today.

Question: Have you ever quit your job? What was your reason—bad boss, crappy pay, minimal growth, better opportunity elsewhere?

I've moved around quite a bit in my career—insert Millennial joke here—and eventually started my own company, but most of the time, when I left an organization, it was due to a lack of professional growth, refusal to change and innovate, and not getting compensated accordingly for being a high performer. Also, growing up, I saw family and friends' parents get laid off after working for an organization their whole careers, and they had to either start over or find a job that would pay their high salary, which could take a long time. As I witnessed this, I came to realize that most (not all) corporations have a bottom-line mentality and need to ensure that they can survive, as well as have to answer to their shareholders, and that if push comes to shove, they're going to protect their best interests over yours, which is understandable. If no one is buying your product or service, how can you keep the lights on?

As you can tell, as an entrepreneur, I'm a little bit more pessimistic about company loyalty, but my mind was ultimately changed when I read the book *Everybody Matters* by Bob Chapman and Raj Sisodia, and my mind was blown! When the global recession occurred around the world (2008-ish), instead of doing what most companies did and lay people off, Chapman (CEO of Barry-Wehmiller [BW]) put people first and was able to save jobs (and not ship them to China under customer pressure) by using voluntary furloughs. Once BW was able to regain their customers and revenue, they paid all their employees back. What a great model. If I were a Gen Zer working there at that time (not possible), I would have told my friends I worked for an amazing company!

The point of this story is that you can gain a competitive advantage as an employer of choice by finding innovative ways to put people first rather than slashing budgets without thinking outside the box. This pandemic is a great litmus test to see how organizations truly value their employees and gives us the opportunity to see whether their corporate mission statements and core values are true or just BS. Putting people first will help you recruit and retain *all* employees, and most likely they will post on Instagram, TikTok, and Snap about how awesome it is to work at your company, which is what you want. (Our Gen Z study found that 83% of Gen Zers admitted that a friend's positive recommendation about a company would be an important factor in deciding to work there.)

According to SHRM, some of the factors that employees identify as the leading cause for job satisfaction are:

- **Respectful treatment of all employees at all levels:** As you'll see in the "Diversity, Equity, and Inclusion" section in this chapter, ensuring that everyone has a seat at the table and gets heard and has equal opportunities is very important to Gen Z. (Over 60% of the Gen Zers surveyed identified diversity and inclusion as an important factor at an organization, and 95% said that it is important for their input to be accepted in the workplace.)

- **Compensation/pay:** When I ask my students what's really important to them when they're looking for a job, the first answer I get is "How much I'll get paid." Then I ask them if they are willing to work a menial type of job for $100,000 a year on a contract for three years, and 90% of them say they wouldn't do it. Obviously pay is very important; it is not the only factor that will retain an employee at your organization, but it should not be overlooked.

- **Trust between employees and senior management:** Our survey of Gen Zers found that 95% think it is important for the leaders of their organization to have integrity and authenticity.

- **Opportunities to use skills and abilities at work:**[46] Our survey found that 97% of Gen Zers preferred to obtain additional job experiences outside of their primary job functions, which can lead to job rotations, temporary assignments (side gigs), and other opportunities to keep them engaged.[47]

In addition, Gallup states, "Employees who use their strengths are more engaged, perform better, are less likely to leave—and boost your bottom line."[48]

The key drivers for turnover are:

- **Employee Dissatisfaction**: Honestly, this is really easy to figure out, even at large organizations, but is your company willing to write a check and spend the resources necessary to get the answer? Also, can the egos of your organization handle the results? As stated earlier, Gallup's "Q12 Employee Engagement Survey" is simple (twelve questions) but truly powerful because it's able to pinpoint employee engagement (or lack thereof) down to the department level and can be anonymous.

  IBM is able to predict with 95% certainty by using AI when an employee is going to quit within six months, which helps managers and leadership intervene to help retain their valuable employees.[49] Some of the predictors include being in the same position for too long, working too much overtime, and the time it takes to get higher pay or a promotion.

- **Better Alternatives**: Yes, the grass is always greener on the other side, but why not create the greener grass in your organization? As more and more Millennials and Gen Zers are entering the workforce with graduate degrees, they tend to get bored more quickly, and by providing a job rotation program in your organization, you keep these employees entertained and more marketable if they ever want to leave. Also, these programs are great because they allow your Gen Zers the opportunity to discover their passion within *your* organization rather than leave and wander corporate America aimlessly. Some of the benefits of a job rotation program as defined by SHRM are "increased productivity, reduced absenteeism and turnover, reduced boredom and complacency, as well as increased innovation and improved work process efficiency."[50] Creating a job rotation program can be tricky from an HR and legal standpoint, so make sure you involve both of these departments from the very beginning of formulating your strategy and program.

- **A Planned Change (pregnancy, graduate school, etc.)**: Why should your employees have to leave if they undertake a planned change such as a pregnancy or going to graduate school? As we've seen during the pandemic, work can happen anywhere and anytime, as long as the work gets done. We would recommend that you take a look at your maternity and paternity leave policies, as well as flextime, which can include time for these employees to go back to school to obtain a graduate degree. Also, what type of program do you have in place once your employee obtains their master's or doctorate degree? A lot of organizations don't *formally* recognize or celebrate their employees' graduations, let alone give them pay raises.

In terms of graduate school, I would recommend talking to managers of employees who attend grad school to see how the employees can apply grad school projects to the organization and be supportive of these projects (easier to do for salaried employees). In addition, managers should be trained and coached on how to support employees who go on maternity and paternity leave. ("Oh, we don't want to promote [insert name here] because he or she is *probably* not going to come back from maternity/paternity leave.")

- **A Negative Experience:** People vent on social media all the time, and the employee experience can have a dramatic impact on retention. Now that we are all connected via social media (especially Gen Z), it's not just about peacefully packing up your stuff, giving two weeks' notice, and driving home. The whole world can see what your employees think about the way they were treated while working at your organization.

Additional predictors of turnover include:

- **Quality of the Employee-Supervisor Relationship:** This can easily be captured in an employee engagement survey, as well as turnover rates within your organization. Does one manager have higher turnover than his or her peers outside the norm (seasonal, layoffs, etc.)? What about exit interview data?

- **Role Clarity and Job Design:** Have you ever gotten a job and, after the first few weeks, said, "Wait a minute, this is not what I signed up for!"? Making sure that your employees are clear about their roles and responsibilities from day one is a big part of being successful. (We'll talk about this in later chapters in greater detail.)

- **Work Group Cohesion:** When someone is not a good fit for your team, it can be cancerous to work group cohesion and productivity. Personality assessments, team-building events, and strong leadership can help alleviate challenges to workplace cohesion.[51]

To review, ways to increase retention include:

- recruitment (the right person for the right job),

- socialization (turnover can be high for new employees),

- training and development,

- compensation and rewards,

- leadership/communication training for supervisors, and

- employee engagement.

THE IMPORTANCE OF DIVERSITY, EQUITY, AND INCLUSION (DEI)

As important as it is for companies to screen an applicant's résumé and background, it's just as important for Gen Z to screen potential employers. With their online savvy, Gen Z will do a full search of the company's website, social media, Indeed, Glassdoor, and any other publicly available information that they can find to see if your company has the qualities and values that align with theirs—and this can sometimes start with diversity, equity, and inclusion (DEI).

Nationally, more than 40% of the population will be minorities and 24% will be Hispanic by 2045.[52] Since this topic is very important to Gen Zers, we're going to spend a good amount of time providing you with information about DEI that is current as of the writing of this book, and we recommend that you continue to keep up with current trends. Also, we'd like to note that the rest of this section is just an overview of each DEI topic, and we recommend that you read further to better understand—you can see resources we pulled from in the footnotes/reference section or use our good friend Google for additional help.

Among the great quotes that have been circulating recently to define diversity and inclusion is one by Vernā Myers (sought-after inclusion strategist and author of *What If I Say the Wrong Thing?: 25 Habits for Culturally Effective People*): "Diversity is being invited to the party. Inclusion is being asked to dance."[53] And a great analogy for equity is, "Equity means that everyone has the opportunity to dance."[54] Our study found that over 60% of Gen Z respondents said that a strong commitment to gender and cultural diversity, which can range from the "Leadership Team" on your company's website to the gender-neutral bathrooms in your office, was an important determinant of the appeal of a workplace.

The Gender Gap

In this section we will talk about ways for organizations to be more inclusive, equitable, and diverse. According to Pew Research Center, in 2020, women made 84% of what men made.[55] Some of the benefits of conducting a pay analysis include values, fairness, talent acquisition and retention, employee morale, and legal compliance.

COVID-19 has been particularly hard on parents, especially women. The Boston Consulting Group (BCG) released a study in May of 2020 that found that 60% of the respondents had no outside help in caring for and educating their children and were now spending an *additional twenty-seven hours* each week on household chores, childcare, and education on top of their household responsibilities before the pandemic. Even though men have been stepping up to help, women are still spending fifteen hours more on domestic labor each week than men, and 50% of the respondents to this survey felt that the quality of their performance at work had decreased as a result of managing these additional responsibilities.[56] Some of the recommendations from this study: communicate, prioritize, be flexible, give working parents the accommodations they need, factor caregiver status into talent evaluations and track impact, and lead with empathy. Even though a lot of Gen Z employees do not have kids yet, setting the tone of being an empathetic and flexible company will help create a culture of trust and inclusion.

Gender Identity

Did you know that "56% of [Gen Zers] know someone who uses a gender-neutral pronoun and 59% believe forms should include options other than 'man' and 'woman'"?[57] In addition, "Globally, 25% of Gen Zers expect to change their gender identity *at least once* during their lifetime."[58] These numbers are staggering in showing how times are changing and evincing that management will need to follow the cultural shift if they want to be inclusive and attract/retain talent.

Before we move on, it's good to list the pronouns that you most identify with, which can be seen here: she/her, he/him, they/them, or ze/hir.[59] To use they/them in the singular tense, consider the following sample: "They are a writer and wrote that book themself. Those ideas are theirs. I like both them and their ideas." While I know this can take some time to adjust to, it is very important to folks in the trans community, as well as future Gen Z employees. People use this on their email signature, LinkedIn profile, Zoom name, or even corporate business cards. A small change can go a long way to truly show that your company values DEI rather than simply including DEI in a fancy mission statement.

Race/Ethnicity/National Origin

Having DEI for your organization is also very important from a racial perspective. "The new census projections indicate that, for youth under 18—the post-millennial population—minorities will outnumber whites in 2020. For those age 18–29—members of the younger labor force and voting age populations—the tipping point will occur in 2027."[60] According to the Pew Research Center, one in four Gen Zers are Hispanic. There is a tremendous opportunity to hire incoming employees from more diverse universities because if you have customers/stakeholders, having a more diverse workforce will help you connect better with them.[61] A study cited in the *Harvard Business Review* found that "a team with a member who shares a client's ethnicity is 152% more likely than another team to understand that client."[62]

While companies have improved their diversity practices over the years, inclusion has still been a challenge to track and measure. The Center for Talent Innovation found that these four components drive inclusion: inclusive leaders, authenticity, networking and visibility, and clear career paths.[63]

We will discuss inclusive leaders in the "Leading Gen Z" chapter but will briefly talk about the other three components here. In terms of authenticity, this study found that "37% of African Americans and Hispanics and 45% of Asians say they 'need to compromise their authenticity' to conform to their company's standard of demeanor or style."[64] The Center for Talent Innovation found that when employees are able to bring their "whole selves" to work, they are "42% less likely to say they intend to leave their job within a year," and 69% of women who off-ramped due to child or elderly care said that they would have stayed at their companies if they'd had flexible work options.[65] Our study found that over half of the Gen Zers surveyed openly admitted that since starting to work from home in light of the pandemic, they have been able to bring their "true self" to work. As you can see, besides sounding like the right thing to do, it makes business sense to create an inclusive culture where people can be themselves.

The key driver for an inclusive workforce is networking and visibility. One of the best professional hacks I teach my undergraduate students is how to network (within and outside an organization) and obtain a mentor. When I teach classes on soft skills, I find only a few students have mentors, which already puts the rest at a disadvantage. The Center for Talent Innovation found that for women and people of color, not getting a sponsor/mentor is one of the factors that holds them back in their careers and can increase the likelihood of them quitting within a year.[66] A sponsor is defined as "a senior-level leader who elevates their protégé's visibility within the corridors of power, advocates for key assignments and promotions for them, and puts their reputation on the line for the protégé's advancement."[67]

Being a multicultural sponsor can have its challenges. The Center for Talent Innovation found that "although 41% of senior-level African-Americans, 20% of senior-level Asians, and 18% of senior-level Hispanics feel obligated to sponsor employees of the same gender or ethnicity as themselves (for Caucasians the number is 7%), they hesitate to take action" because they don't want to face the perception of favoritism or fear that they might not perform. The result is "18% of Asians, 21% of African-Americans, and 25% of Hispanics step up to sponsorship (and 27% of Caucasians)," which can perpetuate a lack of belonging and opportunities.[68] Also, our study found that the type of "leader" that the Gen Zers want to have is a "mentoring coach" over someone who is a task-assigner, fair, or even a technical expert, which shows the importance of mentoring these Gen Zers once they enter the workforce.

Personal Note: I didn't have a true mentor until my MBA program, and he turned out to be my marketing professor. I interned for him because at that time the school did not offer a social media/internet marketing course, and his internship was the only way I could gain one-on-one teaching/mentoring, as well as "real experience." When I have had questions about my career, when I started my consulting business, and at other points, he has been there for me and provided advice. This type of experience has been priceless, and I try to replicate it for students who are trying to start and manage their careers. I encourage you to take the time to mentor at least one person per month—the intrinsic rewards of helping someone creates a myriad of benefits.

The business case for having DEI should be obvious, but here are some quick stats (feel free to look them up in the appendix):

- There is a statistically significant relationship between diversity practices and employee engagement at work for all employees.[69]

- Deloitte found that when organizations utilize *both* diversity and inclusion, employee engagement increases by 101%.[70]

    › The same study found that "if just 10% more employees feel included, the company will increase work attendance by almost one day per year per employee."[71]

- A *Harvard Business Review* study found that "without diverse leadership, women are 20% less likely than straight white men to win endorsement for their ideas; people of color are 24% less likely; and LGBT(QIA)s are 21% less likely," which can have an impact on unmet customer needs/innovating new products.[72]

- Another *Harvard Business Review* study found that employees with inclusive managers were 1.3 times more likely to feel that their innovative potential was unlocked.[73]

- Companies with above-average diversity had 19%-point-higher innovation revenues.[74]

- Another study (by *Economic Geography*) found that culturally diverse leadership teams were more likely to develop new products than homogenous leadership teams.[75]

- When equality is present in a corporate culture, the innovation mindset is six times higher.[76]

- At companies where men are involved in gender diversity, 96% of respondents report progress, and when men are not involved, 30% report progress.[77]

Social Justice

The 2020 murder of George Floyd (among other shootings) sparked protests in major (and minor) cities across the globe. As we saw this all unfold while writing this book, we wanted to know how this would impact Gen Z and employers, so we included a few questions in our national study, which was conducted during late October/late November of 2020, and found the following results:

- The majority of the Gen Zers surveyed said that companies should support social justice issues, DEI, and fairness, while the remaining were split: they didn't know what organizations should do/thought they should do nothing.

- Our study found that 58% agreed that their company did a good job of addressing social justice issues, while 29% remained neutral.

- Lastly, our study found that one in three Gen Zers (34%) surveyed had participated in a protest between May 2020 and November 2020.

The data highlight the importance of social justice to Gen Z (as well as other generations) and should always be at the forefront of leaders' minds and strategic plans.

CONCLUSION

As you can see, a great deal of planning and implementation goes into recruiting and retaining your Gen Z (and all) employees. The pandemic has shifted how we (including Gen Z) will likely prefer to work in the future. Organizations that are proactive and innovative will be the first to recruit and retain top talent as offices open or go remote. We presented a great number of facts and figures in this chapter to help illustrate our points, so please feel free to look them up if you need to sell any ideas to your upper management to help create positive change in your organization.

As stated at the beginning of this section, most recruitment and retention strategies presented in this chapter can work for any generation:

- Create your recruitment marketing plan, and tailor it to your "target market" (see template that follows).

- Measure, measure, measure. Data, data, data. Ensure that you are measuring all the elements stated in this chapter and that you create a dashboard to help you pinpoint areas of improvement.

- Diversity, equity, and inclusion are good for business, good for employees, and good for society. It is recommended that you hire an expert to help you with this effort rather than just add it to an employee's already existing full-time job. (Sound familiar?)

EXERCISES
GEN Z RECRUITMENT MARKETING PLAN

1. What do your employee engagement scores tell you about the level of engagement of your employees? What about Gen Z? If you don't have an employee engagement survey, I recommend using the Q12 survey by Gallup. Also, if you haven't done an employee engagement survey in a while (or ever), be prepared to follow up with action. It can be frustrating to give your true, honest opinion and have the organization do nothing in return.

2. Are your core values, mission, and vision statements visible to your employees by action? For example, your organization says that innovation is a top core value (like every organization), but your employees are still using Windows 95 (a joke, but you get what I mean), or you say that you value DEI, but the same people continue to get the glamour projects.

3. What is your turnover percentage? How does this compare to Gen Z's turnover percentage? Does this turnover align

with your employee engagement scores? Do you tie your supervisors' bonuses/compensation to the employee engagement scores?

Note: Turnover is bound to happen, but make sure you and your employees leave on good terms, and start tracking the boomerang effect of them coming back. (Grass is always greener on the other side.).

4. What does your diversity, equity, and inclusion (DEI) strategy look like? One in four Gen Zers is Hispanic—is your workplace inclusive? Did you include DEI questions in your employee engagement survey? Are you using metrics to measure your DEI progress (diversity of staff, velocity of promotions, engaged employees, increase of sales and innovation, etc.)?

5. How much money per year are you spending on overhead? Can you reduce this cost by partially or completely shifting to remote work? What are the pros and cons of this decision? How will you incubate creativity and innovation virtually? Our recommendation is to base your decision on employee feedback and continue to course-correct and modify if your strategy does not work.

FIVE
WORKING WITH GEN Z

INTRODUCTION

OK—now that we have recruited the top Gen Z employees of today, how do we work with them? Do I need to download TikTok? Do they only communicate via text messages and GIFs? (And what is a GIF?) If I have a different point of view, will they "cancel" or "ghost" me, whatever that means?

I've been doing training and keynotes on how to work with Millennials and Gen Zers for years, and it's funny to hear about organizations that are still trying to figure out how to work with Millennials. As you may recall from the introduction of this book (don't feel bad if you didn't read it; I sometimes skip the introduction section of books too), Millennials started entering the workforce back in 2002, almost eighteen years ago, yet organizations are still trying to figure out how to keep them motivated and work well with them.

We commend you for picking up this book and wanting to get ahead of the curve on trying to understand this generation, which requires education and empathy. We're going to provide information based on *data* and empirical research (not just our anecdotal experiences), explain how they *want* to work, and offer tools you can use to ensure that you are maximizing their workplace engagement and creating an awesome place to work.

WORK ENVIRONMENT PREFERENCES

Before we break down how to work with Gen Z, I think it's important to define what a work environment is. Indeed delineated six factors of a work environment: work hours, company culture, benefits, people, career development, and work space.[1] We cover some of this in the last chapter, but we want to give you a realistic view of what it's like to work with Gen Z on a day-to-day basis and how you can keep them happy and engaged. For the Gen Zers who are reading this book, please don't forget that it's a two-way street, and you should check out the introduction of this book to learn how the other generations prefer to work so you can coexist harmoniously.

Before we jump into how to work with Gen Z, we want to spend some time on Gen Zers' reactions to COVID-19 and how to successfully bring them back to the office. Once we cover the pandemic, we'll go into the different elements of working with Gen Z postpandemic.

Working during and after COVID-19

During the pandemic, I wondered how the *entire* workforce (outside of my bubble) was coping with having to shift overnight to working from home, as well as keeping their teams engaged and positive.

I was asked by an HR professional association to do a presentation on the impact that COVID-19 had on the different generations in the workplace. I only had my point of view because most of my clients were in the trenches of adapting to the pandemic, so I started digging into the internet to see if there were any studies on the impact of COVID-19 on various generations in the workplace. Luckily, Deloitte, McKinsey, and other firms were analyzing this issue as well, and they found some interesting facts. Furthermore, in addition to a study that we conducted two years ago, James and I conducted a national study with a research firm to get a pulse on how Gen Z is faring, as well as glean some information that was missing from the mainstream media, which led us to the following topics. We know that some of this information may be moot by the time this book comes out, but this pandemic may shape the future of work, and we strongly believe that a lot of the information in this subchapter will help you and your organization feel adequately prepared to support your Gen Z employees back in the office or working remotely.

Gen Z Works Remotely—#Blessed?

Gallup offers helpful statistics on how engaged workers can be while working remotely; for instance, the organization notes that "60% to 80% of their time working remotely are the most likely to be engaged."[2] Some of the benefits associated with working remotely are:

- Less commuting (can save employees between $2,500 to $4,000 per year or equivalent of eleven workdays per year if telecommuting half-time[3]).

- Lower carbon footprint (pollution, paper, etc.)— remember how much Gen Z cares about climate change? This is a huge selling point and should be something your organization highlights when folks start going back to work.

- Lower overhead. (Deloitte suggests working from home may "reduce real estate and facilities costs by 10% to more than 20%."[4])

- Telecommuters can sometimes be more productive than their in-office counterparts.[5]

- There is lower turnover when employees are offered remote work.[6]

These stats were all tabulated pre-COVID-19. Part of the challenge for a great portion of us who are working remotely through the pandemic is that we did not choose this, and for the parents out there, we have different responsibilities now (working and teaching remotely) that can impact our behaviors, stress, anxiety, and depression. As you learned from the previous chapter on how Gen Z deals with depression and anxiety, we are now throwing another wrench in the machine.

Deloitte's May/June 2020 report found that working from home would relieve stress for 69% of Millennials and 64% of Gen Z (this was back in May/June 2020),[7] while our survey found 49% of Gen Zers working from home reported increased levels of anxiety, and 49% reported increased levels of depression. In addition, 56% of our Gen Z respondents reported feeling lonely at times while working remotely.

Gallup offers some great definitions and solutions for isolation and loneliness:[8]

- **"Isolation** can be resolved by access to people, decisions, technology and equipment." Deloitte's May/June 2020 survey found that only 53% of Gen Zers and 49% of Millennials reported that employers have offered training, education, and skills development to enable employees to work remotely more effectively. Our study found that 72% of the Gen Zers surveyed were satisfied with their employer's supplied technology to work remotely, which could be attributed to the fact that public health departments around the country (and world) shut down the offices of nonessential businesses, which didn't leave them with much of a choice to provide such technology. Deloitte's data shows a large gap in training and education, which could lead to additional isolation.[9]

- **"Loneliness** reflects a lack of meaningful connection—and the definition of 'meaningful' depends on the worker. Managers need to know that definition for every person on their team and individualize accordingly."

  › One of the tips that Gallup gives to help with this and increase employee engagement (threefold) is that managers should give employees feedback at least a few times a month.

Question to the managers/leaders reading this book: How often did you do virtual town halls and engagement surveys when your folks were shifted to remote work?

What do we do next? Deloitte found that once the COVID-19 era is over, 64% of Millennials and 60% of Gen Zers would like the option to work from a remote location more frequently.[10] Our survey (October/November 2020) regarding the postpandemic work environment found that

- 15% want to work 100% remotely

- 54% want to work remotely at least 50% of the time

The reason our book cover resembles a home office is that we believe that the workplace will permanently be changed after the pandemic is over. Why do we say this? Well, the Band-Aid has been pulled off—employers have been forced to give up control and let their employees work from home. And guess what? We're not kindergarteners, and we can actually be productive and get stuff done. A study by Mercer (an HR and workplace benefits firm) found that 94% of employees said that their productivity was at the same level or higher than before the pandemic began.[11] BCG conducted a global survey of over twelve thousand employees and found similar results—over 75% were able to be as or more productive prepandemic while working remotely, but that number dropped to 51% for collaborating with coworkers, which shows that it would be more difficult for all organizations to be 100% remote in the future.[12]

Leading through COVID-19

When asked if employers trusted their employees to be productive in a remote working environment with minimal monitoring, 59% of Millennials responded yes, compared to 55% of Gen Zers.[13] A study that appeared in *Harvard Business Review* found that "about 40% of supervisors and managers…expressed low self-confidence in their ability to manage workers remotely."[14] In addition, the same study found that workers felt pressured to respond to messages immediately, which could cause anxiety.[15]

One of the main reasons I'm writing another book (a "how-to" guide for first-time leaders) is that managers typically do not get training on how to lead people. Now these managers have to lead remote workers and keep their businesses alive while taking care of their families and becoming K–12 teachers? One of the main challenges leaders face is *motivating* their employees, whether it be remotely or in person. Our study found that 40% of Gen Z employees surveyed had not given their full effort since the pandemic started, while 20% remained neutral and the other 40% said that they had given their full effort. Just think of the productivity lost!

The initial reaction to the pandemic (May/June 2020) can be understood based on Deloitte's report. Millennials and Gen Zers were equally satisfied with how their employer communicated with them during the pandemic (67% for both).

Do employers really *care* about their employees? Do human resources departments actually provide *human* resources? The macro answer seems to be that the majority of Millennials and Gen Z employees are satisfied with their employer's response to the pandemic. Deloitte's May/June 2020 study found that 62% of Millennials and 60% of Gen Zers felt that their employer's actions make them want to stay at the company long-term. In our study 72% of workers agreed that they were proud to work at their company based on their response to COVID-19, and 57% said that they would consider working at their company in the long term based on their organization's response, which may have nothing to do with the response but rather the opportunity to search for a better job.

Deloitte found that 60% of Gen Zers and 58% of Millennials agree that their employer has taken actions to support their mental well-being during the pandemic. A global health study found that 42% of respondents admitted that their mental health had declined since the start of the pandemic, and our study found that 49% of Gen Zers admitted that their anxiety and depression had increased since the start of the pandemic.[16]

Gen Zoomers

So, what's going on with Zoom? I love saying that I've been using Zoom since before it was cool (a whole two years ago) and was very happy to see that the colleges where I teach and my clients use Zoom, but how has video conferencing changed during the pandemic (beyond Zoom's stock price—I wish I had bought some in March)?

I've noticed that many of my students have blank screens during Zoom meetings and hear anecdotally from friends, clients, and professional acquaintances that their employees don't show themselves on their cameras during meetings, so James and I wondered, *What are these people doing while we get to see the blank screen with their name?* Our study found that 54% of Gen Zers show their face most of the time, while 33% show their face half of the time and 13% show their face rarely. We finally have the answer, but you'll have to purchase our field book for an additional $9.95—just kidding! Our study found that when participants did not show their face during a video call, 47% were multitasking, 24% were not presentable, and 18% were not even at their computers! Here's another fun fact: 59% of our Gen Zers said that they had gotten a side gig during the pandemic while working their current job/internship!

Sometimes, for personal reasons or work-related reasons, video calls are not seen as being productive by younger generations, which could explain why they're multitasking or walking away from their computer: "61% of Gen Z workers and 57% of Millennials said the time spent on video calls was hurting their productivity. In comparison, only 35% of Gen X workers and 26% of Baby Boomers felt this way."[17] We thought this was interesting because you can infer from the data that Zoom meetings have not been managed very well and that workers from younger generations would probably like fewer meetings so they can get things done more quickly. I remember hearing from my friends and acquaintances that when the pandemic started and everyone had to work from home, people started scheduling Zoom meetings like crazy because they needed to look busy rather than focusing on task-driven outcomes, which is where Zoom fatigue started. According to a *Harvard Business Review* article, Zoom fatigue can occur because:[18]

- "It force(s) us to focus more intently on conversations in order to absorb information."

- "'Constant gaze' can make us uncomfortable," rather than in-person, where we can look around during a meeting and it won't seem weird.

- "Most of us are staring at a small window of ourselves, making us hyper-aware of every wrinkle, expression, and how it might be interpreted. Without the visual break we need to refocus, our brains grow fatigued."

A recent Deloitte UK report suggests employers there realize a return of £5 (US$6.22) for every £1 (US$1.24) invested in mental health. A 2019 Deloitte Canada report revealed companies with mental health programs in place for three or more years had a median annual ROI of $2.18 (US$1.56) for every dollar (US$0.72) spent.[19]

Remember in chapter 4 when we told you how Gen Z appreciates honesty from their leadership? Well, we took it upon ourselves to poll the Gen Zers in our study to see if they felt their employers were honest and transparent about furloughs and layoffs. Surprisingly, the most definitive answer we received was neutral—meaning that the folks in our study didn't feel one way or another about their organizations being transparent about furloughs and layoffs.

These are all really interesting statistics and help take the pulse of what was happening during May and June of 2020, but James and I wanted to go further and find out what Gen Z employees thought employers needed to do to allow them to safely come back to work. We found that 26% strongly agreed that they looked forward to going back into the office and seeing their coworkers, while 26% felt neutral and 12% were not really looking forward to coming back.

Another factor we examined was the level of effort given by employees to their organizations during the lockdown, and although the results were self-reported (and anonymous), we heard "I have felt more able to bring my true self to work since working from home" and "I look forward to going back to work at a physical office with my colleagues."

We realize that this may be a moot point if some of you pick up this book after 2021, but in a way, it might not be because your company has a chance to create a lasting impression on your young employees by how you handle bringing them back into the workplace postpandemic. To repeat, Deloitte's May/June 2020 report found that 62% of Millennials and 60% of Gen Zers felt their employer's actions make them want to stay at the company long-term, based on their May/June 2020 survey, and our results were similar: 57% of Gen Zers stated that they would stay longer at their current employer due to their employer's reaction and support during COVID-19. In our study, we put forward the statement "Given the overall response to COVID, I am proud to work at my company" and found an overwhelming 72% of the Gen Z respondents agreed with this statement, which is great news for employers.[20]

How will your and your company's actions be remembered?

Making a Difference—in the Workplace

Even though Gen Z is a *serious* generation (as compared to the starry-eyed Millennials), they actually still want to make a difference in the world (52%) but also be independently wealthy (31%). This is very important to note because your company is going to need to start making an impact within the communities that you serve and communicate the hell out of it (only authentically, of course). As an organization or even as an entry-level supervisor, you can achieve this by asking your employees what they are most passionate about outside of work. According to our study, approximately 90% of Gen Zers stated that they are very concerned or somewhat concerned about environmental issues. Doing activities like seeing how many trees you can save by printing less or communicating how your organization is reducing its carbon footprint can help with recruitment and retention of Gen Zers.

#*AlternativeFacts*

As you read in previous chapters, Gen Z is ridiculously reliant on technology and thrives when using it. Our study found that the top characteristic that Gen Zers associated themselves with is being technology-reliant, with multitasking being a close second. These two characteristics are closely tied together and can be detrimental if not used deliberately to achieve organizational goals. We found that a majority of Gen Zers attempted to use authoritative sources when researching online, but 18% of respondents said that they didn't even make the attempt. That means that 1.8 out of 10 Gen Z employees will not even *try* to validate sources when doing research for a potential client or your business processes. And this is self-reported. The Gen Zers who answered this survey question may think that fitness influencers are trustworthy sources. (How many people actually researched to see if these fitness influencers are licensed personal trainers or nutritionists or just trying to sell a product they are paid to promote?)

Going a step further, how does this generation know what an authoritative online source even looks like? When you grow up with the internet, you don't receive internet search training. I didn't get my first *family* computer until I was a junior in high school, so I was a lot more cautious about what I saw on the internet because it was new.

The Pew Research Center conducted a study that found that a large percentage of adults would like to be trained on how to use online resources to find trustworthy information.[21] Some good questions to ask your Gen Z employees when they present you with a work product are:

- Was the data created by a for-profit company? If so, what's its angle in providing the free information?

- Did the company have additional motives or ads on their website to sell products that its report is *proving*?

- What professional certifications do the people writing for the website claim to have? Are they legitimate?

- How was the data collected?

In college we teach students to use *peer-reviewed* articles to validate their research papers, but what happens when they enter the workplace and they don't have access to peer-reviewed articles? And even if they did have access to peer-reviewed articles, would these writings be applicable to their day-to-day jobs? I wrote a peer-reviewed article on leadership while working in the corporate world and sent it to some of my colleagues to read, and they didn't find it as interesting as my professor friends because they don't read academic articles on a daily basis.

I try my best to teach students to question online sources to ensure that what they are providing is valid research so they do not make a mistake when they enter your workplace. The main point of this story is that it's up to companies and managers (and ideally universities) to guide these fresh young recruits on how to conduct proper online research rather than just take a headline they saw on an article and present it to a client. This generation is ridiculously online-savvy, but since they grew up with this information overload and minimal experience pre-internet/smartphone, they need help discriminating the good stuff from the crap that appears online (fake news?).

GEN Z CHARACTERISTICS (ACCORDING TO THEM, NOT US!)

When we asked the question "Which characteristic do you most associate with Generation Z," the responses were all over the map:

- Multitasking (25%)

- Private (19%)

- Technology-Reliant (16%)

- Entrepreneurial (16%)

To help you work with Gen Zers better, we're going to dive into each one of these characteristics.

Multitasking

When I was in high school, my first job was at a bagel bakery, and I used to work the drive-through because it helped pass the time and required a high degree of multitasking. As I got older and looked at job postings and attended resume workshops while in college, multi-tasking was at the top of the list of required skills. But it wasn't until I was introduced to "lean" and "six sigma" by one of my mentors that I learned that multitasking is not good and actually hinders our productivity and that Pomodoro time (doing one task or batch of work for twenty-five minutes, with a five-minute break) can help you accomplish your goals.[22] Some of you reading this may be guilty of multitasking (I am from time to time), but you and your teams need to adjust and show them the benefits of "unitasking," which leads to more productivity. According to psychology professor Larry Rosen, "It takes about 20 minutes or more after processing new information to achieve total resumption of where we were before the interruption."[23]

Private

I remember very clearly (even through jet lag) when I was introduced to Snapchat—I was in the cell phone store getting new phones when I got home from China, and my best friend, who was giving me a ride, told me I should download Snapchat on my phone. When I asked, "What does it do?" he said that I can add cool filters on my face, like a cat or dog. While the novelty of this wore off quickly, I couldn't see myself spending time doing this because of my other commitments in my life but found out later why this app might be appealing: after you post something, it disappears, and when someone screenshots your picture, it alerts you. Gen Zers saw their older siblings and the generation before them get burned by posting everything on social media, so they embraced the privacy that this app provides.

Technology-Reliant

As you saw in our previous chapter on Gen Z and technology, this generation grew up with smartphones, and that has shaped the way they see the world, as well as their expectations of their workplace. Our study found that nearly 30% of the Gen Zers surveyed would not work for a company that would block social media from their work computers/company's Wi-Fi, and 45% admitted that it would be difficult to not have access to their smartphone while at work. In addition, an overwhelming number of the Gen Z respondents (43%) said that being "plugged in" to technology 24-7 can ruin your chances of thinking outside the box and innovating, whereas 22% stated that this action had no impact on innovation.

Entrepreneurial

One of the most common assumptions made about Millennials and Gen Zers is that they're increasingly becoming entrepreneurs or would consider entrepreneurial endeavors as a career path/side gig. Much to our surprise, 47% of the Gen Zers studied said they would start their own business someday, and an additional 36% said they might start one. But is this really that surprising to you? We found that 52% of the Gen Zers we studied wanted to make a positive difference in the world, 86% stated that they are optimistic about their future, the most important requirement for their first job is following their passion (47%), they are ridiculously resourceful finding online resources, they openly admitted to delegating tasks to their peers (67%), and if they want something done right, they'd rather do it themselves (75%).

Based on the characteristics of a successful entrepreneur and what we've discussed in this book, an entrepreneurial mindset can provide a great advantage for large corporations and might create entrepreneurial environments or "intrapreneurs"—those who form new ventures *within* an organization. Even though a lot of our Gen Zers said that they *would* start their own company, that doesn't mean that they *will*, and providing a creative outlet within your organization can give you an edge over competitors, as well as keep this new generation engaged by helping them create something without having to put Mom and Dad's house up for collateral.

Cynical

Even though their Gen X parents were known for being cynical, Gen Zers seem to be more upbeat. This generation grew up during one of the worst recessions in history and now is graduating from college and trying to find a job during a global pandemic, so they have reasons to be cynical, but our study found they were not. We found that 86% of Gen Zers are optimistic about their future and gave their employers positive grades on their responses to the pandemic. They care greatly about the environment and equality and will try their best to ensure that the world will be a better place, long after we're gone.

TRAINING

When we asked how often this generation viewed YouTube or other online streaming videos, 35% stated that they used such a resource multiple times a day, and 30% reported using video streaming services

every day. This can be an incredible outlet for training and development. Keep in mind that short, quick videos are the preference of this
generation, so creating five-minute training videos on how to use SAP,
Oracle, or any other type of software, as well as soft-skills training, is
a great way to utilize this generation's natural talent and love for video
streaming and do-it-yourself (DIY).

Ironically enough, we found that this generation does not want
to be trained exclusively via online training/webinars. (This training
delivery only accounted for 29% preference, compared to face-to-face
or a hybrid training.) Our study found that they actually prefer (51%)
the typical face-to-face two-to-three-hour corporate training (this data
was obtained during the pandemic); 20% of respondents preferred
training to be done partially online, followed by face-to-face reinforce-
ment learning. You may be surprised by this new information, but
it's important to always do surveys and make your training decisions
based on data rather than gut (or a poorly estimated budget).

CONFLICT, GHOSTING (👻), AND CANCEL CULTURE

The past four years have been illuminating in terms of how our culture
and society have shifted. We've seen corporations picking sides when
it comes to social issues, like Nike's response to Colin Kaepernick,
Walmart's decision to stop selling handguns, CVS Health's choice
to stop selling cigarettes,[24] and more. We've also seen the effects of
the #MeToo movement. Over the past few years, we've also seen the
evolution of cancel culture, which can be defined as "a movement to
remove celebrity status or esteem from a person, place, or thing based
on offensive behavior or transgression."[25]

What drove us, as a democratic society, to a place where people are
afraid of voicing their opinions? Dr. Grant Brenner is a board-certified

physician-psychiatrist, an entrepreneur, author, teacher, speaker and not-for-profit board member. He has been featured on a variety of top ranked psychology resources and media as a thought leader and contributor. He wrote a great article in *Psychology Today* explaining the psychological reasoning behind cancel culture; he states:

> Avoidance is a core symptom of posttraumatic stress disorder. Suppression is a good short-term defense, but without access to those experiences, we cannot expand to contain them. If canceling is followed by forgetting, if canceling is a superficial fix and then we move on to the next thing to cancel, we will miss the next stages of the work. From this perspective, cancel culture is "collective ADHD" caused by a need to immediately manage distress through action. We are using spot remover to clean up stains, but no one is deep shampooing the rug...In the longer-run, nuance is needed to work through changes in a country where there is minimal dialogue among competing large group identities. Rather than "Cancel Culture," we would strive for "Cancel And" Culture. Striving for "Cancel And..." is more likely to get us to a better future, rather than impulsively "Marie Kondo'ing" everything which seems problematic and realizing we've thrown out the baby with the bathwater.[26]

As regards canceling at work (*to destroy the force, effectiveness, or validity of or to take away someone's power or cultural capital*), we found:

- 19% of Gen Zers had attempted to or successfully "canceled" someone

- 14% admitted that someone else had attempted to or "canceled" them

While these don't seem like big numbers at first glance, they point to the fact that nearly one in five employees has attempted to "cancel" someone or not show up for an interview. These are some pretty high numbers considering the amount of time and loss of productivity that can occur within an organization. So what should you do?

Before you start freaking out, we thought it might be a good idea to sit down with the expert, and Dr. Brenner graciously agreed to an interview so we could find out what employers should do about employees canceling and ghosting their coworkers in their organizations. We found that "bullying, ghosting, and cancelation speak to underlying attachment insecurity. Disorganized attachment is a form of insecure attachment characterized by chaotic shifting from being overly anxious or preoccupied in relationships to being withdrawn or dismissive, to being fearful or threatened—and sometimes being more secure, safe, and trusting."[27] Furthermore, Dr. Brenner stated that "a significant subset of Gen Zers appear to exhibit a disorganized attachment in relation to professional environments—feeling insecure, not knowing how to get developmental needs met, they appear to be self-contradictory, seeking both to be left alone and tended to with exquisite responsiveness. Put another way, Gen Zers may have room for development of their relationship with work, between their personal identity and emerging professional identity, as earlier experiences may have failed to prepare them adequately."[28]

Dr. Jean Twenge (author of *iGen*) observed this phenomenon at the university level when students started boycotting their universities for allowing conservative speakers to come to campus for a keynote presentation, which she says is contrary to the idea of a university: "College is a place for being challenged by new ideas. Members of iGen [Gen Z] disagree: They see college as a place to prepare for a career in a safe environment."[29] So what happens when these types of students graduate and enter your workplace?

Not many people like dealing with conflict in the workplace, and no group hates it more than Gen Zers. As you saw in the chapter on technology and FOMO, Gen Zers can easily speak their mind and confront people via text message or a Snap, but actually dealing with conflict face-to-face can be incredibly difficult for this generation, and we believe this will be one of the most challenging qualities that this generation will bring to the workplace.

I've delivered keynotes to hundreds of folks across the country on how to work with Millennials and Gen Zers, and I always get one or two people (usually in HR) coming up to me afterward and saying, "You won't believe it…I had someone 'ghost' me for an interview" or "They didn't even show up for the first day of work, even after they signed a contract. Unheard of!"

These comments made for some interesting virtual dinner anecdotes, but is this really happening, or are these incidents outliers? Realizing that this could be a problem for employers, we asked our Gen Zers if they've ever ghosted someone at work or canceled/been canceled. Our results were surprising! For ghosting, we found:

- 17% admitted to being a "no-show" for an interview

- 15% admitted to not showing up for the first day of work

- 11% had quit without notice

- 6% had ceased contacting their coworkers

Recruiters, HR leaders, and functional managers need to be prepared for the possibility of this happening to them and set themselves up to manage this issue proactively by coaching employees on how to deal with conflict in a positive and proactive manner. Also, universities should instill professionalism into their curricula (if they don't already). One study from the National Association of Colleges and Employers found that 89.4% of students considered themselves to be proficient in professionalism, while only 42.5% of employers agreed.[30] High schools and universities need to instill professionalism in their students so that once they graduate and enter the workforce, they'll be ready.

This section is applicable to the majority of Americans who find conflict (or lack thereof) in the workplace to be uncomfortable, stressful, and sometimes downright unproductive. So what does conflict in the workplace look like? Well, "it can be expressed in numerous ways such as insults, noncooperation, bullying and anger. Its causes can range from personality clashes and misunderstood communication to organizational mismanagement."[31] Its various negative effects can include work disruptions, decreased productivity, project failure, absenteeism, turnover, and termination. Emotional stress can be both a cause and an effect of workplace conflict. Can you think of a time when you had a conflict at work and it disrupted your productivity, home life, or even sleep?

Well, it's in our biology as humans to be uncomfortable with conflict. Amy Gallo is an expert in conflict, communication, and workplace dynamics and co-host of HBR's *Women at Work* podcast. She wrote in the *Harvard Business Review*'s guide to conflict that:

> conflict can make us feel like we are giving our power away, and giving away our power triggers our sympathetic nervous system, which then increases your heart rate, breathing rate, your muscles tighten, and your stomach tenses as acid moves into it. Then, we start to panic! When you're panicking, feeling crushed or overwhelmed, the body's response is to be aggressive—punch or push back, or run away and hide. When your brain perceives danger like this, it can be difficult to make rational decisions, which are specifically needed in conflict management situations.[32]

As an extreme extrovert and with "positivity" being one of my top five strengths based on the Gallup CliftonStrengths assessment, I didn't feel that I was properly prepared to deal with conflict in the workplace. It's funny how each place you work has a different corporate culture when it comes to healthy or not so healthy conflict. I remember in one workplace that conflict was dealt with in a passive-aggressive way, while in another company, conflict was addressed head-on and was used as a way to have healthy discourse. Most of these conflict situations derived from a petty email, nuances in meetings, or a project not getting done in a timely manner. But what happens when people won't engage with you in conflict or they go from zero to sixty?

Now that we know what causes us to get extremely uncomfortable, what do we do about it? Well, Gallo found that there are four types of conflict:[33]

1. **Relationship Conflict:** A clash of personalities
   Example: Someone has a really loud voice and may be seen as being confrontational, but that is just the way they talk.

2. **Process**: A disagreement over *how* to carry out a project or task
   Example: You want to use Excel to calculate sales projections for the next quarter, but your boss wants you to use a newer software that could take a longer time to learn and implement. The *how* of getting to the end goal is where the conflict occurs.

3. **Task**: A disagreement over the intended goal of a task or project
   Example: That 25% sales goal is not achievable. The only reason you hit 25% *last year* was that one of your clients had a really good year, but they have scaled back their

spending this year due to the slow growth. You think it should be adjusted to 20%, while your manager thinks it should be 25%.

4. **Status**: A disagreement over who's in charge or who gets credit for the work
   Example: This is a fun one. You did the majority of the work (95%), while your boss commented once or twice but gets credit for your entire project and even gets a bonus, leaving you exhausted and pissed off. Another great example for the Gen Zers reading this book: you are working on a group project for school, and you have two or even three alpha personalities in the group, and they are vying for the leadership position.

The key to dealing with these situations is recognizing which type of conflict is occurring and *why* it is occurring. This adds clarity, and you may be able to address the root cause of the conflict head-on. The reason we say "may" is that not all people like initiating conflict. Gallo also states that there are conflict-seekers and conflict-avoiders—the names speak for themselves, and you probably know which type of person you are in a given situation.

CYBERBULLYING

As we've seen in this generation, bullying (or cyberbullying) has become an ever-expanding problem that starts with kids and social media. I remember that when kids got bullied when I was growing up, only the people who were at school saw the kid get bullied. Now, when kids pick up their smartphones, they can be bullied for the entire world to see 24-7, and people can add comments, likes, and hearts to make it sting even more.

Gen Z has had to deal with the evolution of bullying, and they are very concerned about this in the workplace. Our study found that 70% of Gen Zers are concerned about bullying in the workplace. SHRM defines bullying as "unwelcome behavior that occurs over a period of time and is meant to harm someone who feels powerless to respond." Furthermore, "Social bullying in the workplace might happen by leaving someone out of a meeting on purpose or publicly reprimanding someone."[34] The Workplace Bullying Institute did a study in 2017 and estimated that "61% of U.S. employees are aware of abusive conduct in the workplace, 19% have experienced it, and another 19% have witnessed it." As you can see from the statistics, this topic is on Gen Zers' minds. It will be very important to understand what "bullying" is according to *them*—one employee ghosting another, microaggressions, or flat-out bullying.

GEN ZERS AND MILLENNIALS COLLIDE: BABY BOOMERS AND GEN XERS ARE ROTFL!

While I was helping to shepherd my city through a pandemic, I was constantly reading news articles while at home to keep up-to-date with COVID-19 and noticed that a lot of people were blaming "Millennials" for partying during spring break and causing the pandemic to spread more quickly. I started laughing because people sometimes make the assumption that anyone under forty is a "damn Millennial." Of course, as you now know, folks born in 1995 or later are members of Gen Z.

A lot of my Millennial friends and I have families, and we were trying to figure out how to all of a sudden cope with distance learning, finding toilet paper, making masks out of our old shirts, and watching *Tiger King*—not drinking out of a beer bong on spring break.

This relationship between Millennials and Gen Z is very dynamic because these generations grew up with very different parenting styles.

Millennials grew up believing that they were awesome and that they could accomplish anything because their parents thought so, and they grew up in a great economy—until they graduated college and needed a college degree to work at a department store.

As part of our study, we asked Gen Zers what they thought of their Millennial coworkers. Surprisingly, the response was positive; here are some of the funnier comments:

- "Enthusiastic and energetic when they choose to be, however they often can have short spells of being lethargic, lazy, and/or out of touch with what's going on."

- "As a Generation Zer, my impression of Millennials at work is they are very tech-savvy and creative. Most of the time they work hard, but they often socialize with others throughout the workday."

- "About half are nice and half are arrogant a———."

- "Millennials tend to stick to jobs for financial reasons, even if it is not satisfying or serving a purpose." (We found this quote to be funny because Millennials are known for pursuing their "purpose," but this Gen Zer thinks otherwise.)

- "Millennials are privileged and, in vast numbers, lack the self-awareness to see why they struggle and how their own biases damage others."

- "Anxious and self-sacrificing, thin-skinned, bright, sociable."

As you learned from the previous chapters, Gen Zers grew up with technology and were shuttled around and monitored by their parents;

they grew up in a recession and went to college under a nationalist president who threatened to cancel TikTok and promoted the idea that climate change is a myth—remember that poll earlier that found Gen Z thought climate change was more important than worrying about health care?

Obviously Gen Zers and Millennials grew up during different times with slightly different values, so you may ask: How will they work together? We thought this was a very important question because anecdotally, we've heard from people at conferences and during and after our keynotes, as well as from our mutual acquaintances, grumblings about Gen Z entering the workplace: "What's with this new generation?"

Since we have heard so much about Gen Z entering the workforce, we wanted to ask Gen Zers what they needed from all generations in the workplace and found the following:

- Be open-minded (47%)

- Don't treat me like a child (19%)

- Listen to me (17%)

- Allow me to have a seat at the table (16%)

Again, we found in our study that 51% of Gen Zers expect to change companies three to five times in their career, and 29% expect to change companies two times or fewer. It is important for organizations to be prepared for this, but perhaps you can also transform the employer-employee relationship into an employer-freelancer relationship. A 2021 Pew Research study showed that 16% of Americans have earned money from an online gig platform, and companies that embrace this now will have a competitive edge once this becomes the new normal.[35] We know this may be hard to fathom, but it can be beneficial for both sides. Organizations pay less overhead—in terms of health care, dental, 401(k), tuition reimbursement, and all the stuff we talked about in the last chapter—and Gen Zers will have more flexibility to do what they want. The key is for employer and employee to not burn the bridge when they part ways but rather discuss how to work together in the next stage of the relationship.

CONCLUSION

Gen Zers are either going to school or starting their first job/career during a global pandemic, but they are optimistic about their futures and have found ways to make extra money during this period. This generation is incredibly resilient but will require mentoring and guidance on how to deal with conflict (e.g., ghosting and canceling), interpersonal skills, and working remotely. As you can see from the following chart there is a large gap between the skills that college graduates think they've mastered and what employers are looking for:

Competency	% of Employers That Rated Recent Grads Proficient	% of Students Who Considered Themselves Proficient
Professionalism/Work Ethic	42.5%	89.4%
Oral/Written Communications	41.6%	79.4%
Critical Thinking/ Problem Solving	55.8%	79.9%
Teamwork/ Collaboration	77.0%	85.1%
Leadership	33.0%	70.5%
Digital Technology	65.8%	59.9%
Career Management	17.3%	40.9%
Global/Intercultural Fluency	20.7%	34.9%

Figure 27: "Job Outlook 2018 Survey"
(National Association of Colleges and Employers)[36]

The old production mentality, where being at your desk is defined as working, will not mesh well with this generation, and organizations will have to shift to more of a task mentality when it comes to working with and leading Gen Z. We gave you an intensive breakdown on the benefits of telecommuting, as well as the expectation of Gen Z when they come back to work, so use this as a guide.

COVID-19 has taken a toll on Gen Z's mental health (as well as that of all generations), and providing Gen Zers with resources (therapy, counseling, wellness apps, etc.) will be crucial to their well-being and productivity.

To ensure that Gen Zers stay engaged, provide opportunities for training and growth, such as job rotations and soft-skills development (see Figure 27). Lastly, for the Millennials reading this book, please try to be patient with Gen Z (as *some* Baby Boomers and Gen Xers were with us), and help coach them to be successful.

EXERCISES

1. What's your telecommuting policy postpandemic? (As you've seen from this chapter, the majority of Gen Zers would like to work remotely at least 50% of the time.) Would you consider hiring or keeping 100% remote workers? How much money are you spending on leasing your property?

2. During the pandemic, did you conduct surveys to gauge how employees were doing, what the company should do, etcetera? What was the result? If your organization did this, please don't stop polling workers after the pandemic is over—continue to make data-driven decisions.

3. What mental health resources are available for your employees? Are they being utilized?

4. What does your job rotation program look like? Has it been well-received? If you don't have one, we suggest you develop one and comply with the labor laws in your area. Also, allow side gigs for employees within your organization, as this is what Gen Z prefers, and it will keep them engaged.

5. How often do you provide professional development for your Gen Z employees? Does your training program include conflict management (ghosting, cancel culture, workplace bullying, etc.), DEI, professionalism, communication skills, and business writing?

SIX
LEADING GEN Z

INTRODUCTION

Congratulations, you've made it to the last chapter! The Baby Boomers and some Gen Xers reading this book are probably saying, "Why are they congratulating me?" Meanwhile, the Millennials and Gen Zers get a boost of dopamine and enjoy the praise: "Thanks, bruh!"

Jokes aside, this is an important chapter because an organization cannot run smoothly without employee engagement, which starts with leadership.

One of the major reasons I was drawn to the topic of intergenerational conflict is that it is so prevalent in today's workforce and probably has been since before I was born. Conflict can arise when folks see issues through different lenses, which can cause absenteeism, bullying, passive-aggressive behavior (ghosting), and other consequences, but ultimately the leader is responsible for a harmonious and productive workplace.

A Gallup study found that 50% of employees quit their job to get away from their manager at some point in their career and that "managers account for at least 70% of the variance in employee engagement scores across business units," and only 30% of America's employees are "engaged" in their work.[1] Wow—I just threw a lot of stats at you to support my previous paragraph. To sum it up here: crappy leadership can negatively sway 70% of your workforce, and excellent leadership can inspire 70% of your workforce. Have we created a strong sense of urgency yet?

The leadership book *First, Break All the Rules* by Marcus Buckingham (author of nine books, including two of the best-selling business books of all time) states that "Everyone should be treated as an exception. Each employee has his own filter—his own way of interpreting the world around him. And therefore, each employee will demand different things of you, the manager."[2] This is a profound statement and does not solely apply to Gen Z but rather to all generations. Too often in organizations people are promoted because they excel based on their technical skills (or kiss up to the boss) rather than because they are selfless and lead others. The Center for Creative Leadership (CCL) found that "almost 60% of leaders said they never received any training when they transitioned into their first leadership role."[3] Additionally, the CCL found that "20% of first-time managers were rated as doing a poor job by their subordinates" and "26% of these first-time managers felt that they were not ready to lead to begin with." But since we are focusing in this book on Gen Z, we'll provide you with information on how to effectively lead Gen Zers.

LEADERSHIP VERSUS MANAGEMENT

Now that we've overloaded your brain with a ton of statistics on why you need to provide training for your leaders and how this can jack up your company, let's talk about what leadership really is.

Leadership has been used interchangeably with management and should be properly identified before we go any further. Management is used to create order and consistency within an organization, while leadership is meant to "produce change and movement."[4] The contrast between the two can be seen thus: "if an organization has strong management without leadership, the outcome can be stifling and bureaucratic. Conversely, if an organization has strong leadership without management, the outcome can be meaningless or misdirected for change's sake."[5]

But what's the textbook definition of leadership? We're glad you asked because we have that covered: leadership can be defined as "a process whereby an individual influences a group of individuals to achieve a common goal."[6] Some people follow leaders because they *have* to (are paid to and wouldn't call these people leaders but rather define them as managers), and some people follow leaders because they *want* to. According to Gallup, being a manager is very difficult, and not many people within organizations have the talent required to perform at a high level in a managerial role. Gallup found that only one in ten people possess high talent to manage (lead) others, while two in ten can possess the right talent to lead others if supported by their company with coaching and training.[7] In addition, Gallup found that 82% of organizations miss the mark on high managerial decisions. This could be because when Gallup interviewed managers on why they thought they had been chosen for their current role, the top two responses were:

1. "I was promoted because I was successful in a previous nonmanagerial role."

2. "I have a lot of experience and tenure in my company or field."

So what do these high-talent managers look like? What makes them different from limited-talent managers? Gallup found that high-talent managers excelled in these five "talent dimensions": motivation, assertiveness, accountability, relationships, and decision-making.[8] All of these qualities are important while leading Gen Z. How can you motivate Gen Zers if you don't even know that they are different from Millennials? How can you be properly assertive and hold them accountable if you don't know their working habits? How can you build relationships with them when you yell at them for sending an emoji or GIF in a text message?

MOTIVATING ZOOMERS TO STAY LOGGED ON AND GET MORE ♥S AND 👍S

Before we talk about how to get Gen Z motivated, it's important to do a psychology 101 refresher on motivation. Do you remember our good friend Abraham Maslow and his hierarchy of needs? In order of importance (even though some may overlap), the following needs motivate us during different points in our lives: physiological needs (food, water, warmth, rest), safety needs (security, safety), belonging-ness and love needs (intimate relationships and friends), esteem needs (prestige and feeling of accomplishment), and self-actualization needs (achieving one's full potential, including creative activities).[9]

Quick Exercise: What motivates you to feel like you are *getting* to go to work rather than *having* to go to work? (My answer, to help you get started: For me, it's getting a chance to help create a world of better leaders who, in turn, will help make the people who work for them happier, healthier, and capable of finding greater purpose in their work lives, which I hope will spill into their personal lives. I've found that I am happiest when I'm able to make the most impact on the world.)

So what motivates Gen Z at work? Obviously, there are so many different factors that can influence this answer, but we found that most Gen Zers want to make a positive difference in the world (52%) rather than just getting a job (22%). Also, like Millennials, they want in their first job to follow their passion (47%) over and above doing what they're good at (31%).

So do you as a leader know *each* person's passion and *every* talent intersection on your team? How is your company helping make a positive difference in the world? One of the first things I did when I took over a new team was ask my direct reports the following question during our meet and greet: What are you most passionate about, and how can I help? Once they told me this, I was able to align their passions with the organization's strategic plan and their personal strengths. The results were incredible—they felt empowered, which helped increase engagement; they felt like they were being listened to, probably because they were—I wrote down everything they said; and as we completed their "passion" milestones, I pointed it out and celebrated it with the rest of the staff. From this, we were able to create an "engaged" workforce as measured by Gallup's "Q12 Employee Engagement Survey."

To incorporate Maslow's hierarchy, it seems that Gen Zers' strong motivators fall in the realm of esteem and self-actualization. Interestingly enough, we found that 59% of Gen Zers in our study got a side gig on top of their day job during the pandemic, a decision that could have been fueled by physiological and safety needs. And again, we found that if they had a side gig and if their company paid them more, 70% would quit their side gig and focus primarily on their day job.

Quick Exercise: How can you use the above information to authentically motivate your Gen Zers?

HOLDING ZOOMERS AND LEADERS ACCOUNTABLE

One of the biggest challenges managers and leaders face is setting clear expectations of what is required of their direct employees from day one, as well as the *follow-up* and *coaching* that are necessary to ensure that the employees are getting the support they need to meet their manager's expectations. It's funny because as I look back on my career, I don't recall very clear expectations of and follow-up on what I needed to do to make myself and the organization successful. Of course, we have annual performance reviews where managers have to document how you've performed, which can make functional managers across the country groan because of how arduous they are. But do you receive a copy of a "pro forma" performance review on *day one*? By this I mean a review that asks:

- "What are the goals you want to accomplish this year?"

- "What work product and metrics are required to be a high performer?"

The best onboarding experience I had was with a project overseas. I remember on my first day, when I was still jet-lagged, my manager invited me into a conference room; he had a piece of paper in front of him. He asked me what he could do to help me succeed, what I needed from him as a leader. I was very impressed with this because he had created this document himself—it wasn't an HR document—and he had done this for every new team member who joined the project. He continues to do so to this day. Some of you reading this are probably saying, "I don't have time for that!" Well, this project was one of the hardest projects I've ever had to work on, due to the complexity, the size, and the challenges of working in a foreign country. Even so, my leader found the time to take thirty to sixty minutes on my first day to figure out how to help me and be the best leader for me. David helped create a special culture within our organization where we looked out for each other but still held each team member accountable.

I apologize for the personal rant, but I've worked for some of the most innovative and brilliant companies in the world, and only one manager did this the first day on the job; I carried this practice into my own leadership roles. As you can tell, good and bad leadership can have a ripple effect on newer managers.

Quick Questions: What are the good or bad practices that you've implemented because you had a manager who did the same thing? What do you think the people who work for you will do to carry on your best (or worst) practices?

So what does this have to do with Gen Z? Glad you asked. We have a ton of data on how much time and attention is required to hold this generation accountable, which we'll share with you shortly.

First, it's very important to Gen Zers (98% of them, according to our study) to know what is expected of them on day one. What is typically done on day one when you start at a company? Fill out your I-9, select your insurance plans, hopefully get a sense of the corporate culture. Yes—onboarding and orientation! The Society of Human Resource Management found that:

- "Nearly one-third of all new hires quit their jobs within the first six months."

- "69% of employees are more likely to stay with a company for three years if they experienced great onboarding."

- "New employees who went through a structured onboarding program were 58% more likely to be with the organization after three years."

- "Organizations with a standard onboarding process experience 50% greater new-hire productivity."[10]

Our study found that 37% of Gen Zers would like a few days for onboarding; the next most preferred time span was four hours (28%). If you have a few days for onboarding, build in time to have the conversation with your new employee during the onboarding process. This is a great time for you to set clear expectations for their performance, establish how you plan to measure their work, and determine how often you will follow up and coach them to show that you are invested in their success.

Here's a quick checklist of things that help assure a positive on-boarding experience for Gen Zers:

- Be prepared! I don't know how many times I've seen people lack work to do on day one: "Oh, so I didn't know you were starting today. I guess you can read through the policies and procedures or standards of practice until your boss gets back in the office from vacation."

- Send them COVID-19 safety protocols ahead of time so they feel comfortable and safe. (Remember Maslow's hierarchy of needs?)

- Try to have much of the HR paperwork filled out in advance, but offer support to answer questions as needed. (How many Gen Zers will know which 401(k) or medical plan to choose in their first job?)

- Personalize the onboarding (post-COVID-19). This can include:

  › Post on the company website and LinkedIn welcoming them to the company.

  › Decorate their cubicle.

  › Prepare and print business cards on the first day. (It once took me weeks to get business cards for a position at one company in a country where it was culturally important to have a business card with your title.

Another place I worked had a hard hat with my name on it, which I still have in my office to this day.)

- As the direct supervisor, you should take the new employee to lunch and get to know them as a person.

- Assign them a "buddy" or mentor to help them get assimilated.

- Have the first two to three weeks planned out for them. (This can include training, meet and greets, lunches, etc.)

- Have the employee expectation talk within the first day or two, and talk about what expectations they have of you as a leader.[11]

As stated earlier, some managers fall short on the follow-up and coaching required to ensure that their employees are getting the feedback they need to meet the expectations that the managers outlined on day one. Some of the managers reading this book may say, "I spend a lot of time with my direct reports and still don't get the results I'm looking for." This is very common—a study by Gallup found that only "26% of employees say the feedback they get at work helps them do better work," and only about "two in ten managers instinctively know how to coach."[12] And most importantly, our study found that Gen Zers prefer to have their direct supervisor be a mentoring coach (29%), fair (24%), a friend (15%), a task assigner (12%), and a technical expert (9%). That is, more Gen Zers would prefer to have their boss be a friend than would prefer them to be a technical expert.

The first thing you can do is require managers to train on how to be better coaches, but if that's out of your budget, here are some good ways to start:

- Listen

- Analyze the problem

- Ask relevant, open-ended questions to help them solve the problem on their own

- Practice[13]

Also, it's very important that you know each individual employee's strengths and weaknesses and the best way to approach them. For example, when I've led teams in the past, I have had them take the Clifton StrengthsFinder, and before I meet with them, I pull up their report and try to frame the questions through the lens of their strengths, which helps them better understand the problem and become more excited about solving it. Our Gen Z study found that 56% of those surveyed preferred to have their direct supervisor point out areas for improvement, while 41% wanted them to focus on their strengths. These numbers are surprising, but I think as Gen Zers' careers progress, they'll understand the importance of leaning into your strengths rather than fixating on your weaknesses.

When you meet with your direct reports or manager, how frequent and how long are these meetings? A study published in the *Harvard Business Review* found that on average, managers met with their employees once every three weeks for thirty minutes and that employees who rarely met with their direct reports were disengaged.[14] Our study found that 36% of Gen Zers want to meet with their supervisors at least once per day; another 36%, once per week; and 17%, multiple times per day. It's funny: when I go speak to large groups and tell them these stats, their eyes look like they're going to pop out of their sockets! The good news is that 41% of Gen Zers said they only need to meet for thirty minutes or less, with 39% of them saying they only needed five minutes or less. We know that this deviates from the norm of "once every three weeks," but if you truly want to get the best results out of this generation, you're going to need to change your routine and style. If your employees work remotely, conduct office hours so your team can pop in and out of Zoom or Teams at their leisure for a quick five-minute check-in.

Metrics-Based Accountability

One of my favorite books about teamwork is *The Five Dysfunctions of a Team* by Patrick Lencioni. While each dysfunction is very important and builds on the others, I'd like to talk about the last two dysfunctions, avoidance of accountability and inattention to results, which are directly related to this particular discussion of accountability and expectations.[15]

Lencioni says avoidance of accountability occurs when "the need to avoid interpersonal discomfort prevents team members from holding each other accountable for their behaviors and performance." There were many times when I was just starting out my career where I thought I was doing an exceptional job, and then the employee review process came up, and I'd get an area of improvement mention of being "less gregarious" or "more detail-oriented." I would sit back stunned because my supervisor had waited *all year* to tell me this when I could have fixed it in a heartbeat. What specific work products is he talking about? Why can't I track my professional progress on a dashboard? Wouldn't that be easier for my boss, as well—to be able to see his entire team's performance in a snapshot to help figure out the root cause of performance issues?

Metrics, analytics, key performance indicators (KPIs), and dashboards have been thrown around as the key management buzzwords for the past few years in corporate environments all over the US because organizations do a poor job of designing and implementing systems to track progress. So where do we start? I think it's best to start at the macro level, then zoom in to how Gen Z fits into this management challenge.

First, it's important to have a clear and well-defined strategic plan. What are your management objectives? What does success look like for your department? One of the easiest ways to examine progress and activities associated with the bottom line is to look at sales. I worked in sales in college and was able to see the weekly sales report with metrics on how much we sold, options, etcetera. But how do we compute metrics in knowledge work such as human resources, accounting, or engineering?

As we said earlier, a lot of companies are not good at tracking this unless it's obvious (sales, logistics, etc.), so without a system of metrics, how can you help cultivate this next generation, whose members want to know what's expected of them from day one? The balanced scorecard is a great way to help define your team's KPIs:

- *Customer Satisfaction*—Who pays the bills? If your Gen Zer's position is customer-facing, a customer service survey is an easy way to measure performance. Also, for the HR, accounting, and engineering departments I was talking about earlier, what if the people they work with (internal or external customers) fill out an anonymous customer service survey after they work with them? Can you imagine architects or general contractors getting to fill out a survey about the experience of working with an engineer? Can you imagine the next time you work with accounts payable, getting to fill out a survey on how polite they were?

- *Internal Business Processes*—For this section, only you have the answers for your internal process quality, but let me give you some examples of how I was able to track internal process quality in previous years. While working as a project manager, I created something called a "super comprehensive report" because before I got there, the report wasn't very comprehensive. The IT department and I created a system to track when a purchase order was placed, the due date, when it was delivered to our warehouse, when it was put in crates and delivered to the port, when it was put in a shipping container, when it arrived at the destination port, when it cleared customs, and finally when it arrived in our end user's warehouse. I know this is a lot to measure, but if my shipment were late, it would have cost our company a lot of money, and so this allowed me to do a root cause analysis on delays.

For example, if items were sitting in the warehouse too long, I'd make a call and find out that the crating company was short-staffed. If it took too long to clear customs, I'd contact the logistics supervisor to find out what the holdup was and whether they needed additional information. All of these data points would help create cycle times and, inevitably, a report that I could analyze. Because of my obsession with data, we were able to deliver our project ahead of schedule and under budget by using data to inform our decisions.

- *Employee Morale, Learning, and Growth*—We talked about this a great deal in the retention section, but I still think it's necessary to reiterate its importance. As stated earlier, a manager's compensation (or bonus structure) should have some type of tie or link to the employee engagement scores of the folks they supervise. Remember, managers are responsible for a 70% variance in employee engagement scores, and I find it ludicrous that salaries are not tied to this metric. Also, this is a great way to measure inclusion in your organization, which is very important to Gen Z.

- *Finances*—How does your employee deliver value to the organization? Can you tie your internal process quality to efficiency savings? What about your employee engagement scores to lower turnover and absenteeism? How about meeting project deadlines that would inevitably cost the company money if they were missed (similar to my example)? Being able to tie the other three categories (customer satisfaction, internal process quality, and employee engagement) to your bottom line will provide justification for promoting the right employees to make your organization more profitable.[16]

As you can see, these types of metrics help your Gen Zers know how they will be measured, are transparent, and, if explained correctly, will allow them to see how they fit into the bigger picture of your organization.

BUILDING STRONG RELATIONSHIPS

One of the things I miss most about working for a large organization is the comradery and friendships that are built while working in the trenches. I remember when I was a project manager, we had one area that was behind schedule, and I was asked to help them out. Once I got a chance to make an assessment of their progress, I realized that the schedule was more compressed than I thought, and it would require me to put in more time in the office and less at home. Everything was good on the home front, and I couldn't let my coworkers down, so I volunteered to put in the extra time because I saw my coworkers as a family, which is what we were.

One of my fondest memories of working overseas was Thanksgiving. Unfortunately, quite a few of my coworkers were not able to fly back for Thanksgiving, so my wife and I hosted all of these folks at our apartment complex, along with other expats, and tried our best to make everyone feel at home and not bummed out about missing their own families. Almost every year since (excluding during the pandemic), my wife and I host some of these same friends and coworkers at our house for a "Friendsgiving" and relive our glory days working together overseas on that project.

We know that it's common sense to build strong relationships with your coworkers. Indeed found the following benefits: increased satisfaction with your career, feeling more comfortable doing presentations, being more productive, receiving moral support to meet deadlines, and higher retention rates.[17]

But how can we implement this? Do we say, "Hey, bruh, will you be my BFF?" The real world doesn't work this way, and the following checklist[18] is a good place to start:

- **Be present:** I don't know how many times I've been in meetings or even one-on-one conversations, and the person I'm talking to is on their phone. If I know the person and it's part of their deal, I understand, but if you're just getting to know someone, this can be a bridge-burner before you even leave the castle. (This tip is for the younger generations reading this but can be helpful for *all* generations—we're all guilty!) Our study found that 95% of Gen Zers think it is important for their managers to have integrity and authenticity. As we've seen in the news, this generation has little tolerance for BS and will call you to the carpet (or cancel you) if you don't meet their high standards.

- **Understand your strengths and weaknesses:** We talked about this earlier, but if you're trying to build relationships with folks you don't know very well at work but you hate talking to people, map out a game plan to put you in a situation in which you know you'll succeed (e.g., volunteer for a special project you're passionate about). Also, I may sound like a broken record, but the Clifton StrengthsFinder Assessment is a great people hack to get to know yourself and the people you work with in a very short amount of time.

- **Ask questions and listen:** One of the things I was terrible at right out of college was listening. I would sometimes get bored with what the person was saying and interrupt them, or I would guess what they were trying to say (and was wrong 50% of the time). This is really important because people love to talk about themselves, and you can glean a ton of useful information by observing and listening to people. If face-to-face/virtual conversations don't work, pay more attention to the IMs, emails, and texts from your Gen Zers. As you saw before, around 50% of Gen Zers may text you an emoji or GIF, so google it or ask your kids what it means to ensure that you understand what they are saying.

- **Offer assistance:** Helping out a coworker from a different department is not only excellent customer service, but it will also help build relationships and political capital within your organization. If you are managing Gen Zers, understand that they may be right out of college and may not even know the basics about personal finance, graduate school, and anything else related to "adulting." Pointing out a good book or resource that can help them out will go a long way.

- **Keep your commitments and apologize when you make a mistake:** We'll talk about trust in the next section, but it's very important as a leader/manager to *consistently* keep your word, especially to the Gen Zers who report to you. By consistently keeping your word, you'll be able to gain trust. Also, admitting when you make a mistake shows vulnerability, which is one of the key elements to authenticity. Our study overwhelmingly found that Gen Zers strongly preferred leaders to be authentic and have integrity. What is an "authentic" leader? "Authentic" is a leadership buzzword that has been floating around the hallways of corporate America for quite some time, so we'll quickly define it for you. Bill George, former CEO of Medtronic and now a Harvard Business School professor, conducted a study of successful leaders from a variety of industries and found that authentic leaders exhibit five dimensions:[19]

  › **Pursuing purpose with passion:** "Authentic leaders must first understand themselves and their passions… without a real sense of purpose, leaders are at the mercy of their egos and narcissistic vulnerabilities." The younger generations, as well as others, have a great BS meter and can become easily disengaged if their leaders are only serving themselves rather than the organization and may even call out the leader in a town hall. (Uh oh—you may be next!) It is your calling as a leader (and actually your job!) to have other people follow you based upon your organization's strategic objectives (standard MBA jargon), such as increasing sales by 25% this quarter or doubling customer satisfaction year over year. If this sounds boring (and it kind of does), why don't you show how you make an impact in the community with the products or services that you provide?

Our study found that 51% of the respondents stated that the social impact and the mission of the company would be an important factor in working there, with another 31% responding "maybe." It is the leader's job to ensure that they are communicating their vision and passion within the organization to help enable a strong corporate culture. I have worked at some of the most incredible companies in the world, and you could tell how passionate some people were about what the organization was trying to achieve, as well as the fact that some people weren't passionate because their leaders didn't convey the impact correctly (or at all). When employees see that their leader is just one stop away from their next job/company, they tend to become disengaged and might look for a job elsewhere. Toyota has a saying of bringing the "whole self" to work, rather than just using their hands on the assembly line.[20]

> **Leading with heart:** "Having passion for your work, compassion for your people, empathy for the people you work with, and the courage to make difficult decisions." If you are a leader reading this book, I want to ask when the last time was you put yourself in someone else's shoes. Part of the purpose of this book is to create empathy for Gen Z. If you're not a Gen Zer, you didn't grow up with a smartphone. You don't know what it's like to be cyberbullied or be constantly

connected to social media as a teenager, so much so that you lose sleep and self-confidence. We're hoping that by understanding Gen Z (putting yourself in their shoes), you will be a more effective leader and help leverage their current talents into helping achieve your strategic objectives, as well as providing coaching for interpersonal skill development. Gallup's book *Strengths Based Leadership* backs this claim of leading with heart with a study that found that followers need four things from their leaders: trust, compassion, stability, and hope.[21]

› **Establishing enduring relationships:** "People today demand personal relationships with their leaders before they will give themselves fully to their jobs. They insist on access to their leaders, knowing that trust and commitment are built on the openness and depth of relationship with their leaders. In return, people will demonstrate great commitment to their work and loyalty to the company." Our study found that Gen Zers feel overwhelmingly positive about meeting with their leaders on a face-to-face basis. And guess what? They want to meet with their leaders every day or once a week (83%) for at least five to thirty minutes (85%)! The days of meeting with your subordinates once a month or every couple of weeks are disappearing. To get a head start, you should probably schedule this time on your calendar, preferably during your downtime. These meetings should also include time for constructive feedback. Our study found that most Gen Zers wanted their managers to coach them based upon areas for improvement (72%), while others wanted to be coached based on their strengths (24%)—only 2% wanted to be left alone.

› **Demonstrating self-discipline:** "Authentic leaders know competing successfully takes a consistently high level of self-discipline in order to produce results. They set high standards for themselves and expect the same from others." Ironically, Gen Z prefers to know what is expected of them from their first day on the job. Our study found that 91% of the participants thought that it was important or very important that they know what is expected from them on day one. But what percentage of employees actually know what is expected of them? Per Gallup, only six in ten employees strongly agree that they know what is expected of them at work. So if you are a leader of Gen Zers, take the time to clearly articulate what is expected of them from the first day of the job and hold them accountable, preferably with objective measurable metrics or KPIs.

EMPOWER INNOVATION

Did you know that the top in-demand skill for 2020 (as rated by LinkedIn) is creativity (same as in 2019)?[22]

I remember reading in business school about how Google gave their employees 20% of their workweek to work on special projects that would benefit Google (outside of their day-to-day job duties), which made me put this company on an MBA pedestal: I can set aside 20% of my workweek (one full day) to work on whatever I want as long as it benefits the company? That's awesome! Google stated that only 10% of its employees utilized this policy, and it doesn't operate within management oversight. Former head of Google HR Laszlo Bock says about this policy, "It operates somewhat outside the lines of formal management oversight, and always will, because the most talented and creative people can't be forced to work."[23]

Before we continue to discuss how you can lead your Gen Zers to creative nirvana, let's define the difference between creativity and innovation. One of the most simplistic and accurate ways to delineate the two is "creativity is about coming up with the big idea. Innovation is about executing the idea—converting the idea into a successful business."[24]

OK, now that we have these two defined and delineated, how important are they to leading Gen Z at work? One of the questions we asked in our survey was "Would you prefer to have some portion of your time at work to reflect and innovate?" Surprisingly, we had an overwhelmingly positive response: 81% of Gen Zers responded yes; Millennials have had similar responses. (In a Deloitte study, 78% of Millennials stated that a prospective employer's reputation for innovation can strongly influence their decision to work there.)[25] I can sense some managers being very uncomfortable with giving up this amount of autonomy/time in allowing Gen Zers to create videos on TikTok. (Let's not stereotype!)

As we discussed earlier, accountability and expectations from day one are very important, so how do you *implement* this type of policy? As you just read, Google doesn't have their managers formally oversee this policy, and only 10% of their employees use it. Giving your employees time to innovate is not a policy shift but rather more of an organizational cultural shift. How does your company approach creativity and innovation? As published in *Harvard Business Review*, researchers Vijay Govindarajan and Chris Trimble found from their study of thousands of Fortune 500 executives that their companies are "better at generating ideas (average score of six[out of ten]) than they are at commercializing them (average score of one)."[26] Also, another study published in the *Harvard Business Review*, conducted by Laura Sherbin and Ripa Rashid, found that employees with inclusive managers were 1.3 times more likely to feel that their innovative potential had been unlocked.[27] So back to leading your Gen Zers: if you give them time to reflect and innovate, make sure you help eliminate roadblocks in order to help them execute their ideas.

We're going to take a COVID-19 detour here. How many of you reading this book had to shift the way your business's or your organization's operations worked? How quickly did you ideate and implement? This pandemic has forced businesses to adapt to survive, but it's going to be interesting to see if any innovation or adaptability will stick once the pandemic is over. PwC conducted a study on remote work during COVID-19 and found that "83% of employers now say that remote work has been successful for their company, compared to 73% in their June 2020 survey."[28] In addition, the same study found that only 13% of executives are willing to let go of the office for good.[29] Lastly, 55% of employees would prefer to work remotely at least three days a week.[30]

BE A MORE "INCLUSIVE" LEADER

Now that we've talked about the *benefits* of creativity and innovation, let's talk about how you can be an inclusive manager/leader for Gen Zers. We spoke earlier about the importance of creating a culture of inclusion; an article in the *Harvard Business Review* written by market research giant Gartner's teammates (Lauren Romansky, Mia Garrod, Katie Brown, and Kartik Deo), lists the following components (of the Gartner Inclusion Index) as being necessary to create an inclusive workplace: fair treatment, integrating differences, decision-making, psychological safety, trust, belonging, and diversity. Also, the researchers recommend that leaders:[31]

- **Listen**

   If you are a manager or leader within an organization, it's
   important to be a "facilitator" during team meetings and
   not let the loudest person (which used to be me when I was
   younger, or maybe it still is!) get all the airtime. An article in
   SHRM focused on engaging introverts recommends meeting
   with introverts before or after the meeting to get their
   feedback (one-on-one), giving them time to prepare for the
   meeting, and avoiding calling on them during the meeting.[32]

   And whether or not your Gen Zer is an introvert or
   extrovert, our study found that 95% of respondents said
   that it was important to have their input *be accepted* in the
   workplace. (67% rated this as extremely/very important,
   while the remaining said it was moderately/slightly
   important.)

- **Create a Psychological Safe Space**

   How many times in your career have you heard, "Don't be
   afraid to speak up," but when you do, the office politics
   interfere ("Ooooh, that's going to make Jamie's department
   look bad!"), or a sarcastic coworker says something smart
   and you don't speak up again? Some folks need to muster
   a lot of confidence before speaking up during meetings
   (or even one-on-one conversations), so please create a safe
   environment for people to speak in. (Think back to our
   safe space section in chapter 2.) Also, I remember back in
   school seeing teachers or professors chastise students for
   asking certain questions or look at them like they were
   idiots, which is contrary to how we learn. For example,
   in the book *Facilitating Learning with the Adult Brain*

in Mind, education experts and professors Kathleen Taylor (Saint Mary's College of California) and Catherine Marienau (DePaul) state that "in terms of learning, when the brain is scared, it has a foot on the brake; when it is curious, it has a foot on the accelerator." One of the comments I get from my Gen Zer students is how inclusive my classroom is and how they feel comfortable speaking up without being judged by their peers or me.

Note: We're not advocating for the workplace to be an arena in which you are stepping on eggshells if you disagree with a coworker's idea but rather one in which people disagree respectfully and refrain from launching personal attacks. Also, if you don't like someone's *idea,* please bring data to the table to support your claim against theirs and see it as a coaching opportunity, rather than an opportunity to make someone feel uncomfortable and flaunt your intelligence out of insecurity or narcissism.

- **Trust**

I don't know about you, but I've worked for one or two micromanagers in my day and vowed not to again. The feeling you get is that you have to run *every* decision by them because it needs to be done their way, which is completely illogical in most cases because there is more than one route to the finish line. Some of the common themes of micromanagement are hovering, depleted autonomy, stifling employee creativity and growth, and inevitable turnover.[33] Gallup found the following symptoms of a micromanagement culture:[34]

> "Boss-obsessed rather than customer-obsessed"—Would your boss rather cater to themself or your customer (internal/external)?

> "Every decision must be approved by the manager"— You see this a lot in government environments (and usually for good reason, due to the fact that they are spending tax dollars), but there's got to be room for employees to think for themselves; be there as their parachute so they don't fail and break rules.

> "Quick turnover of talented experts"—I've seen plenty of star performers leave organizations because they were micromanaged, not compensated correctly, or not appreciated.

> "Constant project bottlenecks due to excessive meetings, gatekeeping and stakeholders"—So about that: one of the funniest things I've seen in organizations that will not be named is that you have people who schedule meetings to talk about meetings, without agendas, action items, accountability/follow-up, which is a waste of time and resources, which is reflected in our Gen Z study when we asked, "How useful are meetings in getting things done?" Of the respondents, 39% found them useful, but a whopping 32% replied that they were indifferent. Why are we having meetings if they're not useful? *Because the boss says so* or the person running the meeting is not skilled enough to create value for those participating in the meetings.

- **Lead by Fair Treatment and Integrating Differences**
  Taking advice and implementing feedback is what helped
  make me successful. There is so much knowledge out
  there that one cannot know everything, and being humble
  enough to take advice and implement feedback will benefit
  you and your organization tenfold. For example, while
  working overseas, I knew how to do business within my
  organization a certain way, but since I was in a different
  country, I constantly asked for the opinions of the local
  employees in that country to ensure that I was interpreting
  the reality of the project correctly. If I hadn't done this, I
  would have had a false sense of security in regard to the
  project schedule and vendor performance.

Being a leader is truly a thankless job. A *great* leader will take credit
for when things go wrong and give credit to their team when things
go right. These are the types of behaviors that make employees feel
emotionally safe and want to continue working at your company for
the long term. But too many times, we see managers (I'm not going
to call these people "leaders") throw their team under the bus when
things go wrong and take credit when their team performs well. As
we stated earlier in this chapter, the number one trait Gen Z wants
in their manager is "mentoring/coaching." Would a mentoring coach
throw their team under the bus or give them credit?

Also, one of the questions I ask during my leadership training for
my clients is "What is your preferred way of being recognized, publicly
or privately?" and "Do you know your direct reports' recognition
preferences?" These are important questions to ask before you start
praising people at work because otherwise the praise can have the
opposite effect.

TRANSFORMATIONAL VERSUS TRANSACTIONAL LEADERSHIP

Next, we'd like to talk about transformational leadership versus transactional leadership. These are some of the most common leadership theories we talk about in graduate school courses, and you'll most likely recognize them as you continue to read (if you haven't fallen asleep yet!).

Laissez-faire leadership, listed as a subset of transactional leadership, is pretty much how it sounds—an absence of leadership intervention. This has proved to be the *least* effective leadership model and can actually create the least engagement among employees as they are ignored and free to do what they like and manage their careers, as well as day-to-day problems (according to Gallup).

Transactional leadership provides rewards and punishments based upon effort and performance (the carrot and the stick). For example, you get chewed out at work because you forgot to do your TPS reports correctly.

Aside from TPS reports (*Office Space* joke), leaders who practice transformational leadership exhibit the following four components, as seen in the popular text *Leadership: Theory and Practice* by Peter Northouse and made famous by Bernard Bass:[35]

- **Charisma**: "Leaders who act as strong role models for followers…provide them with a vision and a sense of mission."

  Example: The CEO presents a vivid picture of next year's goals and celebrates the milestones of the year.

- **Inspiration**: "Communicates high expectations to followers, inspiring them through motivation to become committed to and a part of the shared vision in the organization."

Example: The CEO's speech shows how the work that the employees do helps change their communities, and even the world.

- **Intellectual Stimulation:** "Stimulates followers to be creative and innovative and to challenge their own beliefs and values as well as those of the leader and the organization."

  Example: The corporate culture is to challenge all employees and be there to help them before they fail or accept failure as innovation.

- **Individualized Consideration**: "Act as coaches and advisers while trying to assist the followers in becoming fully actualized."

  Example: Mary is treated differently than Karen, and so on. Each person is treated fairly, but with an individual approach. This is one of the most challenging (and rewarding) tasks of being a leader because it takes a lot of time to get to know each employee's strengths and quirks, but it's part of the job, and the intrinsic reward of seeing each team member grow is the best perk of being a leader. Also, personality tests (such as the StrengthsFinder) are a quick way to get to know your employees very well and cater to their strengths.

Why is transformational leadership important? Well, Bass's study found that employees exert extra effort under transformational leaders, compared to transactional leaders. Ironically enough, the laissez-faire style of leadership extracts the *least* effort from employees, while intellectual stimulation extracts the most effort, with charisma and individualized consideration close behind. This is important because our study found that Gen Zers value having a leader who is a coach and a mentor over one who is fair or a technical expert. In addition, Goleman's study found that the leadership styles that positively impact a corporate culture the greatest (in order) are authoritative ("Come with me," self-confidence, empathy), affiliative ("People come first," focus on building relationships and communication), and coaching ("Try this," develop future leaders, and help employees develop long-term strengths).[36]

SITUATIONAL LEADERSHIP

Yes, I know we put a few theories in here for you, but we wanted to give you a tool set that you can use when this new generation enters your workplace (though the book can also serve as a great refresher for you to use with the other generations that you lead).

Situational Leadership was developed by legendary business consultants Paul Hersey and Ken Blanchard, and their newest model, Situational Leadership II, consists of two different behavioral styles as defined from the leader's point of view. The first style is directive behavior, which consists of helping followers by providing direction on how to complete a task, including goals, evaluation of goals, deadlines, roles, and how to get there. Next, leaders can exhibit supportive behavior, which consists of helping "group members feel comfortable about themselves, their coworkers, and the situation." This includes showing social and emotional support, as well as "asking for input, solving problems, praising, sharing information about oneself, and listening."[37] According to this model (as described in Northouse's *Leadership*), followers with low competence and high commitment (typically green employees) require large amounts of direction and less exertion of supporting behavior. The model also states that when followers start to gain more competency, they can get bored, and so the leader must exhibit a coaching style to motivate them by giving encouragement and soliciting follower input.

This is how the workplace used to be. Millennials and Gen Zers have ended the days when you could just tell people what to do and walk away, and our study supports this. Again, Gen Zers prefer to have a **mentoring coach** as a leader, with **fairness** being ranked as the number two priority at 29%, and being a **task assigner** ranked at number three (10%). For Gen Zers, autonomy to do their job and having input be accepted were important or very important (84% for both).

The next leadership style is the supporting approach, which requires leaders to "take a high supportive, low directive style. The leader does not focus exclusively on goals but uses supportive behaviors that bring out followers' skills around the goal to be accomplished. This includes listening, praising, asking for input, and giving feedback."[38] As you can see, Gen Z will need both coaching and supporting leadership, but you must make sure that you are clear about what the end goal is so that the Gen Zers do not get lost. Our study found that giving Gen Zers time to disconnect or unplug will encourage creativity and innovation. It may behoove you to have mandated retreats or companywide "unplug" Fridays (for one hour—we're not crazy!) to ensure that they are supported.

CONCLUSION

As we've discussed in this section, Gen Z will require more frequent tag-ups, but not for very long. They expect their leaders to be transparent and authentic, have integrity, and be a mentor/coach to them in times of need. DEI and the environment are very important to this generation, so make sure you continue to stay current with these topics and that your organization continues to address these issues and communicate your progress in a clear and transparent manner.

Most of the content in this chapter can be applied to all generations at work, and our best advice for you (if you're a leader in any organization—work, church, nonprofit, PTA, etc.) is to listen, be open-minded, cater to your employees' personalities and strengths, utilize metrics for accountability, and be compassionate. As stated earlier, Gallup defines the four basic needs of followers as hope, stability, compassion, and trust. How will you address these four needs for your team today?

EXERCISES

1. What's your onboarding process for new employees? Do you have a personalized approach to onboarding (shout-out on social media or internal newsletter, personalized T-shirt or company gear, etc.)? Does your organization assign them a "buddy" to help them get situated? What role does the new employee's manager play in this process? Do you have at the very minimum a two-week plan/agenda for your new employee? This plan can include prescheduled meet and greets, lunches, and training.

    As stated above, we recommend utilizing the following questions once your new employee has had time to get settled:

    a. What type of leadership style do I need to have to help make you successful?

    b. What are your short-term and long-term goals?

    c. What professional development opportunities are you interested in?

    d. What are your pet peeves? I'd like to avoid them.

    e. What makes you excited about coming to work?

    f. Do you have everything you need to be successful (computer, software, ergonomic workstation, location of files, etc.)?

    g. Here are the expectations of this role. Do you have any questions or need any clarification?

2. Do you provide leadership training for all supervisors? Does this training consist of EQ, communication (emails, body language) and facilitation (meetings, training, etc.), leadership styles, coaching, trust and vulnerability, employee engagement/motivation, DEI, etcetera?

3. Do your managers utilize metrics to measure performance and accountability for their employees?

4. How often do the managers in your organization meet with their direct reports one-on-one? Our data says that Gen Z prefers to meet multiple times per week for five minutes or so. How do you do this virtually? (Schedule a five-minute calendar invite? No, office hours are a great tool. Have people pop in for a few minutes; this can be moderated easily utilizing VTC software.) Do you provide actionable feedback without being rude or engaging in personal attacks?

5. Do you empower your team, or are you a micromanager? (Trust but verify is OK.)

6. What are your core values? Are your core values visible to your team, by actions and words?

7. Utilize personality assessments (such as the Clifton StrengthsFinder) to ensure that each manager knows how to get the best out of their employees.

CLOSING THOUGHTS

We have provided you with a ton of facts and figures throughout this book to help explain how the impact of parenting on Gen Z helped mold them to become who they are in the workplace, as well as the impact technology had on them growing up. In addition, we provided you with the results from our national survey focused on how Gen Z prefers to be recruited, retained, and led and how they will shape the workplace until the next generation (Gen Alpha) comes along. It is important to remember that we don't want to stereotype *any* generation but rather to understand the environment that each generation grew up in and how it might contribute to any type of miscommunication or friction that could arise at work.

We had the chance to catch up with Simon Sinek, which brought us full circle, back to where the idea for this book began, and asked him what advice he would give to folks who interact with Gen Z, based on what he's seen since the "Millennial" video. His thoughts are below:

- We need to have empathy—not how do I feel in their shoes, but how do "they" feel in their shoes—and to understand and appreciate what they are going through, whether you agree or not. The responsibility of any leader is to learn, practice, and teach empathy, which all takes time, and there's no app for that. Hard skills and human skills (not soft skills)—it's now our responsibility as leaders and organizations to teach these "human skills."

- The Great Resignation is an indictment of corporate culture and leadership that has been mediocre for quite some time, and the reason why people haven't quit their job up until this point is because the "great unknown" is much scarier than sticking with a mediocre leader/ organization. And when the pandemic hit and people got furloughed or lost their jobs, they realized that they were still alive—it sucked and stress was high, but the "great unknown" became a little less scary and seemed more appealing than staying for their mediocre boss.

- Companies that invest in culture and leadership have a massive competitive advantage—people don't want to leave if their employer cares about them; they want to be seen and understood. The number of community gatherings that create a sense of belonging, like church (from 62% in 2008–2010 to 49% in 2018–2020) and bowling leagues, has been steadily decreasing.[1] Employees still need this sense of belonging, community, and purpose and look to their employers to provide these elements.

Next Steps: We recommend that you continue to build relationships with Gen Zers in your life or at the office and have an open mind. Gen Z is an incredible generation: they grew up during the recession (and are now growing up amid a global pandemic), are ridiculously tech-savvy, and care about the environment and equality for all. It makes us feel good that this next generation is going to be a cohort of folks who will continue to push for change and have a realistic outlook on life. Please utilize all the exercises provided in this book, and continue to revise them as the world changes. We wanted to create a book that you can write in and immediately start using in your workplace or even at home with your Gen Z family members. Thank you very much for reading our book, and we hope you feel confident working with and leading this amazing and emerging generation.

—*Santor and Rocco*

ENDNOTES

INTRODUCTION

1   Sinek, Simon. "The Millennial Question." YouTube. 2016. https://www.youtube. com/watch?v=vudaAYx2IcE.

2   Stepler, Renee. "Divorce rates up for Americans 50 and older, led by Baby Boomers." Pew Research Center. 2017. https://www.pewresearch.org/fact-tank/2017/03/09/led-by-baby-Boomers-divorce-rates-climb-for-americas-50-population/.

3   "College Is Just the Beginning: Employer's Role in the $1.1 Trillion Postsecondary Education and Training System." Georgetown University Center on Education and the Workforce. 2015. https://cew.georgetown.edu/cew-reports/college-is-just-the-beginning/.

ONE

1   Seemiller, Corey, and Meghan Grace. *Generation Z Goes to College.* Hoboken, NJ: John Wiley & Sons, 2016.

2   "Americans Name the Top Historic Events of Their Lifetimes." Pew Research Center. December 2016. https://www.pewresearch.org/politics/2016/12/15/americans-name-the-top-historic-events-of-their-lifetimes/.

3   Image created from US Census Bureau Data. Census.gov. http://www.census.gov.

4   "Greenbook Part 1." Federal Reserve Board. 1980. https://www.federalreserve.gov/monetarypolicy/files/fomc19801118gbpt119801112.pdf.

5   Hewson, Marilyn A., and Michael A. Urquhart. "Unemployment continued to rise in 1982 as recession deepened." Bureau of Labor Statistics. 1983. http://www.bls.gov/opub/mlr/1983/02/art1full.pdf.

6   US Department of Labor. "Registered Apprenticeship National Results Fiscal Year 2020 10/01/2019 to 9/30/2020." Retrieved from https://www.dol.gov/agencies/eta/apprenticeship/about/statistics/2020.

7   Parker, Kim, and Ruth Iglienk. "What We Know About Gen Z So Far." Pew Research Center. 2020. https://www.pewresearch.org/social-trends/2020/05/14/on-the-cusp-of-adulthood-and-facing-an-uncertain-future-what-we-know-about-gen-z-so-far-2/.

8   Miller, Dennis. *The Rants*. New York: Doubleday, 2000.

9   Image created from survey results by Nishizaki, Santor, and James DellaNeve.
     "National Survey of Gen Z at Work." 2021.

10   Ibid.

11   Fry, Richard. "Gen X the only generation to rebound from Great Recession
     in wealth." Pew Research Center. 2018. https://www.pewresearch.org/fact-
     tank/2018/07/23/gen-x-rebounds-as-the-only-generation-to-recover-the-wealth-
     lost-after-the-housing-crash/.

12   Nishizaki, Santor, and James DellaNeve. "National Survey of Gen Z at
     Work." 2021.

13   Ibid.

14   Christnacht, Cheridan, and Briana Sullivan. "About Two-Thirds of 23.5 Million
     Working Women with Children Under 18 Worked Full-Time in 2018." US
     Census Bureau. 2020. https://www.census.gov/library/stories/2020/05/the-choices-
     working-mothers-make.html#:~:text=Working%20mothers%20make%20up%20
     a%20significant%20part%20of,U.S.%20Census%20Bureau%E2%80%99s%20
     2018%20American%20Community%20Survey%20%28ACS%29.

15   Rajalakshmi, J., and R. Thanasekaran. "The Effects and Behaviours of Home Alone
     Situation by Latchkey Children." *American Journal of Nursing Science* 4, no. 4
     (August 2015). https://doi.org/10.11648/j.ajns.20150404.19.

16   "Crime and Justice Atlas 2000." Justice Research and Statistics Association. 2000.
     https://www.jrsa.org/projects/Crime_Atlas_2000.pdf.

17   "NCIC Missing Person and Unidentified Person Statistics for 2007." Federal
     Bureau of Investigation. 2007. https://archives.fbi.gov/archives/about-us/cjis/ncic/
     ncic-missing-person-and-unidentified-person-statistics-for-2007#4.

18   Haidt, Jonathan, and Greg Lukianoff. *The Coddling of the American Mind*. New
     York: Penguin Publishing Group. 2018.

19   Skenazy, Lenore, Jonathan Haidt, Glenn Garvin, Baylen Linnekin, Ronald Bailey,
     Emilie Dye, and Eric Boehm. "The Fragile Generation." *Reason Magazine*. 2017.
     https://reason.com/2017/10/26/the-fragile-generation/.

20   Howe, Neil. "Meet Mr. and Mrs. Gen X: A New Parent Generation." American
     Association of School Administrators. n.d. http://www.aasa.org/SchoolAdministra-
     torArticle.aspx?id=11122.

21   "Parenting in America." Pew Research Center. 2015. https://www.pewresearch.org/
     social-trends/2015/12/17/parenting-in-america/.

22   Ibid.

23   Holley, Lynn, and Sue Steiner. "Safe Space: Student Perspectives on Classroom
     Environment." *Journal of Social Work Education*. 2005. 41(1), 49–64. DOI:
     10.5175/JSWE.2005.200300343.

24   Haidt and Lukianoff. *The Coddling of the American Mind.*

25   Ibid.

26   Holley, Lynn, and Sue Steiner. "Safe Space: Student Perspectives on Classroom Environment."

27   Rose, Flemming. "Safe Spaces On College Campuses Are Creating Intolerant Students." HuffPost. 2017. https://www.huffpost.com/entry/safe-spaces-college-intolerant_b_58d957a6e4b02a2eaab66ccf.

TWO

1   Davis, Dominic. "24 Slang Words Teens Are Using in 2020, and What They Mean." Insider. 2019. https://www.businessinsider.com.au/slang-words-terms-teens-current-2019-8.

2   Mendoza, Jordan. "Gen Z terms on TikTok confusing you? Cheugy, no cap and more defined." *USA Today.* 2021. https://www.usatoday.com/story/life/2021/06/04/gen-z-slang-tiktok-confusing-you-cheugy-no-cap-defined/5281473001/.

3   Nulsen, Charise R. "35 Trending Gen Z Slang Phrases and What They Mean." FamilyEducation. 2021. https://www.familyeducation.com/slang/35-gen-z-slang-phrases-all-parents-should-know.

4   Mendoza. "Gen Z terms on TikTok confusing you?"

5   Nulsen. "35 Trending Gen Z Slang Phrases."

6   Davis. "24 Slang Words Teens Are Using in 2020."

7   Nulsen. "35 Trending Gen Z Slang Phrases."

8   Davis. "24 Slang Words Teens Are Using in 2020."

9   Ibid.

10   Ibid.

11   Ibid.

12   Ibid.

13   Ibid.

14   Ibid.

15   Ibid.

16   Enan, Robin. "The Newest Teen Slang Trends of 2021." FamilyEducation. 2021.

17   Davis. "24 Slang Words Teens Are Using in 2020."

18   Ibid.

19   Nulsen. "35 Trending Gen Z Slang Phrases."

20 Ibid.

21 Enan. "The Newest Teen Slang Trends."

22 Ibid.

23 Nulsen. "35 Trending Gen Z Slang Phrases."

24 Ibid.

25 Ibid.

26 Twenge, Jean M., and Heejung Park. "The Decline in Adult Activities Among U.S. Adolescents, 1976–2016." *Child Development* 90, no. 2 (September 2017): 638–654. https://doi.org/10.1111/cdev.12930.

27 Fry, Richard, Kim Parker, and Amanda Barroso. "Majority of Americans Say Parents Are Doing Too Much for Their Young Adult Children." Pew Research Center. October 2019. https://www.pewresearch.org/social-trends/2019/10/23/majority-of-americans-say-parents-are-doing-too-much-for-their-young-adult-children/.

28 Horowitz, Juliana M., Anna Brown, and Rachel Minkin. "A Year Into the Pandemic, Long-Term Financial Impact Weighs Heavily on Many Americans." Pew Research Center. March 2021. https://www.pewresearch.org/social-trends/2021/03/05/a-year-into-the-pandemic-long-term-financial-impact-weighs-heavily-on-many-americans/.

29 "Young Americans & Money Bank of America/USA TODAY Better Money Habits® Report Fall 2016." Bank of America. 2016. https://about.bankofamerica.com/content/dam/about/report-center/bmh/2016/BOA_BMH_2016-REPORT-v5.pdf.

30 Robertson, Steve. "How to Raise a Gen Z Kid." *ParentMap.* 2018. https://www.parentmap.com/article/generation-z-how-raise-kids.

31 Johnston, Lloyd D., Patrick M. O'Malley, Richard A. Miech, Jerald G. Bachman, and John E. Schulenberg. "Monitoring the Future National Survey Results, 1976-2015." The University of Michigan Institute for Social Research. 2016. http://www.monitoringthefuture.org/.

32 Henderson, Tim. "Why Teens Still Don't Want to Get a Driver's License." The Pew Charitable Trusts. 2017. http://www.pewtrusts.org/en/research-and-analysis/blogs/stateline/2017/03/03/why-teens-still-dont-want-to-get-a-drivers-license.

33 Kamin, Mir. "Why Don't Teens Want Their Driver's Licenses Anymore?" Alpha Mom. n.d. https://alphamom.com/parenting/teens-dont-want-drivers-licenses-anymore/.

34 Johnston et al. "Monitoring the Future."

35 Williams, Jess. "Are my generation really as boring as everyone says?" *New Statesman.* 2014. https://www.newstatesman.com/comment/2014/09/kids-are-alright-0.

36 Robertson. "How to Raise a Gen Z Kid."

37   Lenhart, Amanda. "Teens, Technology and Friendships." Pew Research Center. 2015. https://www.pewresearch.org/internet/2015/08/06/teens-technology-and-friendships/.

38   Heywood, Wendy, Kent Patrick, Marian Pitts, and Anne Mitchell. "'Dude, I'm Seventeen…It's Okay Not to Have Sex by This Age': Feelings, Reasons, Pressures, and Intentions Reported by Adolescents Who Have Not Had Sexual Intercourse." *The Journal of Sex Research* 54, no. 9 (December 2015): 1207–1214. https://doi.org/10.1080/00224499.2015.1092105.

39   Anderson, Monica. "6 facts about teen romance in the digital age." Pew Research Center. 2015. http://www.pewresearch.org/fact-tank/2015/10/01/6-facts-about-teen-romance-in-the-digital-age/.

40   "NCHS Data Brief, Number 308, Declines in Births to Females Aged 10–14 in the United States, 2000–2016." Centers for Disease Control and Prevention. 2018. https://www.cdc.gov/nchs/data/databriefs/db308.pdf.

41   White, James E. *Meet Generation Z: Understanding and Reaching the New Post-Christian World.* Grand Rapids, MI: Baker Publishing Group, 2017.

42   Department of Human and Health Services - The Substance Abuse and Mental Health Services Administration. "Key Substance Use and Mental Health Indicators in the United States: Results from the 2018 National Survey on Drug Use and Health." (2018). Retrieved from https://www.samhsa.gov/data/sites/default/files/cbhsq-reports/NSDUHNationalFindingsReport2018/NSDUHNationalFindingsReport2018.pdf.

43   Twenge and Park. "Decline in Adult Activities Among U.S. Adolescents."

44   Johnston et al. "Monitoring the Future."

45   Looze, Margaretha de, Quinten Raaijmakers, Tom T. Bogt, Pernille Bendtsen, Tilda Farhat, Mafalda Ferreira, Emmanuelle Godeau, et al. "Decreases in adolescent weekly alcohol use in Europe and North America: evidence from 28 countries from 2002 to 2010." *European Journal Of Public Health* 25, no. 2 (April 2015): https://doi.org/10.1093/eurpub/ckv031.

46   "Office of Juvenile Justice and Delinquency Prevention: The Decline in Arrests of Juveniles Continued Through 2019." https://ojjdp.ojp.gov/sites/g/files/xyckuh176/files/media/document/DataSnapshot_UCR2019.pdf.

47   Ibid.

48   Ibid.

49   Ibid.

50   Puzzanchera, Charles. "Dating Violence Reported by High School Students, 2017." Office of Juvenile Justice and Delinquincy Prevention. 2020. https://ojjdp.ojp.gov/library/publications/dating-violence-reported-high-school-students-2017.

51   Ibid.

52   Planty, Michael, Lynn Langton, Christopher Krebs, Marcus Berzofsky, and Hope
     Smiley-McDonald. "Female Victims of Sexual Violence, 1994-2010." Department
     of Justice. 2016. https://www.bjs.gov/content/pub/pdf/fvsv9410.pdf.

53   Baum, Katrina, and Patsy Klaus. "Violent Victimization of College Students,
     1995–2002." Department of Justice. 2005. https://bjs.ojp.gov/content/pub/pdf/
     vvcs02.pdf.

54   Planty, Michael, Lynn Langton, Christopher Krebs, Marcus Berzofsky, and Hope
     Smiley-McDonald. "Female Victims of Sexual Violence, 1994-2010."

55   Twenge and Park. "Decline in Adult Activities Among U.S. Adolescents."

56   Parker, Kim, and Ruth Iglienk. "What We Know About Gen Z So Far." Pew
     Research Center. 2020. https://www.pewresearch.org/social-trends/2020/05/14/
     on-the-cusp-of-adulthood-and-facing-an-uncertain-future-what-we-know-about-
     gen-z-so-far-2/.

57   Ibid.

58   Pannoni, Alexandra, and Glen Justice. "Get Experience at Top Tech Companies
     as a Teenager." USNews.com. 2016. https://www.usnews.com/high-schools/arti-
     cles/2016-08-08/get-experience-at-top-tech-companies-as-a-teenager.

59   Fry, Richard, Paul Taylor, Wendy Wang, Daniel Dockterman, and Gabriel
     Velasco. "College Enrollment Hits All-Time High, Fueled by Community College
     Surge." Pew Research. 2009. https://assets.pewresearch.org/wp-content/uploads/
     sites/3/2010/10/college-enrollment.pdf.

60   Schmidt, Erik. "School Enrollment: College Down, Graduate School Up." Census
     Bureau. 2019. https://www.census.gov/library/stories/2019/12/school-enrollment-
     college-down-graduate-school-up.html.

61   Barroso, Amanda, and Stella Sechopoulos. "Employment, workforce participation
     of college grads fell amid COVID-19." Pew Research Center. 2021. https://www.
     pewresearch.org/fact-tank/2021/05/14/college-graduates-in-the-year-of-covid-19-
     experienced-a-drop-in-employment-labor-force-participation/.

62   Christianson, John. "How to Talk to Your Kids About Money When You Have a
     Lot of It." Harvard Business Review. 2016. https://hbr.org/2016/09/how-to-talk-
     to-your-kids-about-money-when-you-have-a-lot-of-it.

63   Horowitz, Juliana M., Anna Brown, and Rachel Minkin. "A Year Into the Pan-
     demic, Long-Term Financial Impact Weighs Heavily on Many Americans." Pew
     Research Center. 2021. https://www.pewresearch.org/social-trends/2021/03/05/a-
     year-into-the-pandemic-long-term-financial-impact-weighs-heavily-on-many-
     americans/.

64   "Prolonged Housing Crisis Diminishes Confidence in the American Dream, 2015
     Housing Matters Survey Finds." MacArthur Foundation. 2015. https://www.
     macfound.org/press/press-releases/prolonged-housing-crisis-diminishes-confi-
     dence-american-dream-2015-housing-matters-survey-finds.

65 Larrimore, Jeff, Jenny Schuetz, and Samuel Dodini. "What are the Perceived Barriers to Homeownership for Young Adults?" Finance and Economics Discussion Series 2016-021. Washington: Board of Governors of the Federal Reserve System. 2016. http://dx.doi.org/10.17016/FEDS.2016.021.

66 Gayeski, Diane. "Will Generation Z Even Care about HR Technology?" Society of Human Resource Management. 2015. https://www.shrm.org/resourcesandtools/hr-topics/technology/pages/will-generation-z-even-care-about-hr-technology.aspx.

67 Bryant, Natalie B., and Rebecca L. Gomez. "The teen sleep loss epidemic: What can be done?" *Translational Issues In Psychological Science* 1, no. 1 (2015). https://doi.org/10.1037/tps0000020

68 Jiang, Jingjing. "How Teens and Parents Navigate Screen Time and Device Distractions." Pew Research Center. 2018. https://www.pewresearch.org/internet/2018/08/22/how-teens-and-parents-navigate-screen-time-and-device-distractions/.

69 "GPA & Emotional Effects of Sleep Deprivation on High School Students." American Academy of Sleep Medicine—Association for Sleep Clinicians and Researchers. January 2020. https://aasm.org/poor-sleep-can-negatively-affect-a-students-grades-increase-the-odds-of-emotional-and-behavioral-disturbance.

70 Hutchens, Lauren, Teresa M. Senserrick, Patrick E. Jamieson, Dan Romer, and Flaura K. Winston. "Teen driver crash risk and associations with smoking and drowsy driving." *Accident Analysis & Prevention* 40, no. 3 (May 2018): 869–876. https://doi.org/10.1016/j.aap.2007.10.001.

71 Nishizaki and DellaNeve. "National Survey of Gen Z at Work."

72 Ludden, Alison, and Amy Wolfson. "Understanding Adolescent Caffeine Use: Connecting Use Patterns With Expectancies, Reasons, and Sleep." *Health Education & Behavior.* 2010. 37(3), 330–342. https://doi-org.lib.pepperdine.edu/10.1177/1090198109341783.

73 Gussone, Felix. "America's Obesity Epidemic Reaches Record High, New Report Says." NBC News. 2017. https://www.nbcnews.com/health/health-news/america-s-obesity-epidemic-reaches-record-high-new-report-says-n810231.

74 "NCHS Data Brief, Number 288, October 2017." Centers for Disease Control and Prevention. 2017. https://www.cdc.gov/nchs/data/databriefs/db288.pdf.

75 Ibid.

76 "Insulin Restistance and Diabetes." Centers for Disease Control and Prevention. https://www.cdc.gov/diabetes/basics/insulin-resistance.html.

77 "Rates of new diagnosed cases of type 1 and type 2 diabetes on the rise among children, teens." National Institutes of Health. 2017. https://www.nih.gov/news-events/news-releases/rates-new-diagnosed-cases-type-1-type-2-diabetes-rise-among-children-teens.

78 "National Diabetes Statistics Report," 2017. Centers for Disease Control and Prevention. US Department of Health and Human Services. 2017.https://dev. diabetes.org/sites/default/files/2019-06/cdc-statistics-report-2017.pdf.

79 Feinberg, Andrea T. "Prescribing Food as a Specialty Drug." NEJM Catalyist. April 10, 2018.

80 "NCHS Data Brief, Number 288, October 2017." Centers for Disease Control and Prevention. 2017.

81 Purcell, Jim. "Meet the Wellness Programs That Save Companies Money." *Harvard Business Review.* 2016. https://hbr.org/2016/04/meet-the-wellness-programs-that-save-companies-money.

82 Mozaffarian, Dariush. "Want to fix America's health care? First, focus on food." The Conversation. 2017. http://theconversation.com/want-to-fix-americas-health-care-first-focus-on-food-81307.

83 Geiger, A.W. and Leslie Davis. "A growing number of American teenagers—particularly girls—are facing depression." Pew Research Center. July 2019. https://www. pewresearch.org/fact-tank/2019/07/12/a-growing-number-of-american-teenagers-particularly-girls-are-facing-depression/.

84 Shrier, Abigail. "To Be Young and Pessimistic in America." *Wall Street Journal.* May 2021. https://www.wsj.com/articles/to-be-young-and-pessimistic-in-america-11621019488.

85 Dennis-Tiwary, Tracy. "Satisfy Your Craving for Human Contact." The Garrison Institute. 2017. https://www.garrisoninstitute.org/blog/satisfy-your-craving-for-human-contact/.

86 Dennis, Tracy. "Can't Fight This Feeling: Technology and Teen Anxiety." *Psychology Today.* 2017. https://www.psychologytoday.com/us/blog/more-feeling/201712/can-t-fight-feeling-technology-and-teen-anxiety.

87 Tate, Emily. "Anxiety and depression are the primary concerns for students seeking counseling services." Inside Higher Ed. 2017. https://www.insidehighered.com/news/2017/03/29/anxiety-and-depression-are-primary-concerns-students-seeking-counseling-services.

88 Reetz, David R., Carolyn Bershad, Peter LeViness, and Monica Whitlock. "The 2016 Association for University and College Counseling Center Directors Annual Survey." 2017. https://www.aucccd.org/assets/documents/aucccd%202016%20 monograph%20-%20public.pdf

89 Johnston, et al. "Monitoring the Future."

90 American College Health Association. "American College Health Association-National College Health Assessment Fall 2017 Reference Group Executive Summary." https://www.acha.org/documents/ncha/NCHA-II_FALL_2017_REFERENCE_GROUP_EXECUTIVE_SUMMARY.pdf.

91 Ibid. Graphic mastered from source data for clarity. 2018.

92 Ibid. Graphic mastered from source data for clarity. 2018.

93 Healthy Minds Study. "College-aged students experiencing suicidal ideation from 2007 through 2017."2016-2017." Retrieved from https://healthyminds-network.org/.

94 Ibid.

95 Ibid.

96 Ibid.

97 Ibid.

98 Ibid.

99 Lin, Liu yi, Jaime E. Sidani, Ariel Shensa, Ana Radovic, Elizabeth Miller, Jason B. Colditz, Beth L. Hoffman, Leila M. Giles, and Brian A Primack. "Association between social media use and depression among US young adults." *Depression and Anxiety* 33, no. 4 (2016): 323–331. https://doi.org/10.1002/da.22466.

100 Sheikh, Mashhood A., Davy Vancampfort, and Brendon Stubbs. "Leisure time physical activity and future psychological distress: A thirteen year longitudinal population-based study." *Journal Of Psychiatric Research* 101 (June): 50–56. 2018. https://doi.org/10.1016/j.jpsychires.2018.02.025.

101 Goldfield, Gary S., Marisa Murray, Danijela Maras, Angela L. Wilson, Penny Phillips, Glen P. Kenny, Stasia Hadjiyannakis, et al. "Screen time is associated with depressive symptomatology among obese adolescents: a HEARTY study." *European Journal of Pediatrics* 175, no. 7 (July 2016): 909–19. https://pubmed.ncbi.nlm.nih.gov/27075014/.

THREE

1   Judson, Mel. "Crazy Stories of People Who Died Playing Pokemon Go." Ranker. n.d. https://www.ranker.com/list/insane-pokemon-go-death-stories/mel-judson.

2   Puiu, Tibi. "Smartphone is millions of times faster than NASA's 1960s computers." ZME Science. 2021. https://www.zmescience.com/research/technology/smart-phone-power-compared-to-apollo-432/.

3   Paterson, Jim. "The Good, The Bad, and What's Next." ERIC. 2017. https://files.eric.ed.gov/fulltext/EJ1142215.pdf.

4   Baker, Zachary G., Heather Krieger, and Angie S. LeRoy. "Fear of missing out: Relationships with depression, mindfulness, and physical symptoms." *Translational Issues in Psychological Science* 2, no. 3 (2016): 275–282. https://doi.org/10.1037/tps0000075.

5   Greenberg, Marco. "How Long Can You Unplug?" Society of Human Resource Management. 2021. https://www.shrm.org/executive/resources/articles/pages/unplug-for-deep-thinking-marco-greenberg.aspx.

6   Baker, Krieger, and LeRoy. "Fear of missing out." 275–282.

7   Alter, Adam L. *Irresistible*. New York: Penguin Press, 2017.

8   Ibid.

9   Dr. David Greenfield in discussion and email correspondence with the author. April 11, 2019.

10 Ibid

11 Snaidero, Nicolas, and Mikael Simons. "Myelination at a glance." *Journal of Cell Scientists* 127, no. 14 (July 2014): 2999–3004. https://doi.org/10.1242/jcs.151043.

12 Makinodan, Manabu, Kenneth M. Rosen, Susumu Ito, and Gabriel Corfas. "A Critical Period for Social Experience–Dependent Oligodendrocyte Maturation and Myelination." *Science* 337, no. 6100 (September 2012): 1357–1360. https://doi.org/10.1126/science.1220845.

13 Greenfield in discussion and email correspondence with the author.

14 Doreen Dodgen-Magee in discussion and email correspondence with the author. April 17, 2019.

15 "How Heavy Use of Social Media Is Linked to Mental Illness." *The Economist*. May 18, 2018. https://www.economist.com/graphic-detail/2018/05/18/how-heavy-use-of-social-media-is-linked-to-mental-illness.

16 Rosen, Larry D., Mark Carrier, Jonathan A. Pedroza, Stephanie Elias, Kaitlin M. O'Brien, Joshua Lozano, Karina Kim, et al=. "The Role of Executive Functioning and Technological Anxiety (FOMO) in College Course Performance as Mediated by Technology Usage and Multitasking Habits." *Psicologia Educativa* 24, no. 1 (2018): 14–25. 2017. https://doi.org/10.5093/psed2018a3.

17 Schechner, Sam. "France Takes On Cellphone Addiction With a Ban in Schools." *Wall Street Journal*. 2018. https://www.wsj.com/articles/france-takes-on-cellphone-addiction-with-a-ban-in-schools-1534152600.

18 Nishizaki and DellaNeve. "National Survey of Gen Z at Work."

19 Ibid.

20 Brown, E. A. "Study: Mobile phone ban may boost test scores." Education Daily. (2015). 48(101), 1–2.

21 Doreen Dodgen-Magee in discussion and email correspondence with the author. April 17, 2019.

22 Johnston et al. "Monitoring the Future."

23 Nishizaki and DellaNeve. "National Survey of Gen Z at Work."

24 Ibid.

25 Ibid.

26 Doreen Dodgen-Magee in discussion and email correspondence with the author. April 17, 2019.

27 Ibid.

28 Auxier, Brooke, and Monica Anderson. "Social Media Use in 2021." Pew Research Center. 2021. https://www.pewresearch.org/internet/2021/04/07/social-media-use-in-2021/.

29 Ibid.

30 Craig, Barbara. "Electronic Distractions and Child Maltreatment." Military Families Learning Network. 2014. https://militaryfamilieslearningnetwork.org/wp-content/uploads/2018/11/Wired-for-Distractions-Webinar-handout.pdf.

31 Greenfield in discussion and email correspondence with author. April 11, 2019.

32 Brewer, Judson. *The Craving Mind*. New Haven: Yale University Press, 2017.

33 "How Heavy Use of Social Media Is Linked to Mental Illness." *The Economist*.

34 Greenfield in discussion and email correspondence with the author. April 11, 2019

35 Ibid.

36 Doreen Dodgen-Magee in discussion and email correspondence with the author. April 17, 2019.

37 Mischel, Walter, and Ebbe B. Ebbesen. "Attention in delay of gratification." *Journal of Personality and Social Psychology* 16, no. 2 (1970): 329–337. https://doi.org/10.1037/h0029815.

38 Conway, Jan. "Wine consumption worldwide, 2020." Statista. January 2021. https://www.statista.com/statistics/232937/volume-of-global-wine-consumption/.

39 Nishizaki and DellaNeve. "National Survey of Gen Z at Work."

40 Goleman, Daniel. "What Makes a Leader?" *Harvard Business Review*, January 2004. https://hbr.org/2004/01/what-makes-a-leader.

41 University of British Columbia. "Programs that teach emotional intelligence in schools have lasting impact". ScienceDaily. July 2017. www.sciencedaily.com/releases/2017/07/170712072752.htm.

42 "Stress in America™ Generation Z." American Psychological Association. n.d. https://www.apa.org/news/press/releases/stress/2018/stress-gen-z.pdf.

43 Jaret, Peter, and Lynn Rossy. "What is Mindfulness?" Mindful.org. 2020. https://www.mindful.org/what-is-mindfulness/.

44 Ibid.

45 Doreen Dodgen-Magee in discussion and email correspondence with the author. April 17, 2019.

46 "Depression and anxiety: Exercise eases symptoms." Mayo Clinic. n.d. https://www.mayoclinic.org/diseases-conditions/depression/in-depth/depression-and-exercise/art-20046495.

47 "How Much Sugar Do You Eat? You May Be Surprised!" New Hampshire Department of Health and Human Services. Health Promotion in Motion. n.d. https://www.dhhs.nh.gov/dphs/nhp/documents/sugar.pdf.

48 Goleman. "What Makes a Leader?"

49 Geng, Yayuan, Weihua Zhao, Feng Zhou, Xialoe Ma, Shuxia Yao, Rene Hurlemann, Benjamin Becker, and Keith M. Kendrick. "Oxytocin Enhancement of Emotional Empathy: Generalization Across Cultures and Effects on Amygdala Activity." *Front Neurosci.* 2018. https://doi.org/10.3389/fnins.2018.00512.

50 Greenfield in discussion and email correspondence with the author. April 11, 2019.

FOUR

1   "State of the American Workplace." Gallup. 2017. https://www.gallup.com/workplace/238085/state-american-workplace-report-2017.aspx.

2   "2016 Human Capital Benchmarking Report". Society of Human Resource Management. 2016. https://www.shrm.org/hr-today/trends-and-forecasting/research-and-surveys/Documents/2016-Human-Capital-Report.pdf.

3   Glynn, Sarah Jane, and Heather Boushey. "There Are Significant Business Costs to Replacing Employees." Center for American Progress, April 27, 2017. https://www.americanprogress.org/article/there-are-significant-business-costs-to-replacing-employees/.

4   "2016 Human Capital Benchmarking Report". Society of Human Resource Management.

5   "Global Millennial Survey 2020." Deloitte. 2020. https://www2.deloitte.com/gr/en/pages/about-deloitte/articles/MillennialSurvey2020.html#:~:text=The%202020%20report%20consists%20of,midst%20of%20the%20worldwide%20pandemic.

6   "Election Week 2020: Young People Increase Turnout, Lead Biden to Victory." Tufts (CIRCLE). 2020. https://circle.tufts.edu/latest-research/election-week-2020.

7   Matos, Kenneth, Ellen Galinsky, and James T. Bond. "National Study of Employers." Society for Human Resource Management. 2017. https://www.shrm.org/hr-today/trends-and-forecasting/research-and-surveys/Documents/National%20Study%20of%20Employers.pdf.

8   "Flexible Schedules." US Department of Labor. n.d. https://www.dol.gov/general/topic/workhours/flexibleschedules.

9   Matos, Calinsky, and Bond. "National Study of Employers."

10 University of California, Riverside—Human Resources. "Compressed Workweek—Non-Exempt Employees." n.d. https://hr.ucr.edu/document/work-life-form-alternative-work-schedule-agreement-non-exempt-employee.

11   Mann, Annamarie, and Amy Adkins. "What Star Employees Want." Gallup. June 10, 2022. https://www.gallup.com/workplace/231767/star-employees.aspx.

12   Fry, Richard. "5 facts about Millennial households." Pew Research. 2017. https://www.pewresearch.org/fact-tank/2017/09/06/5-facts-about-millennial-households/.

13   "Living with a parent is the most common young adult living arrangement for the first time on record." Pew Research Center. 2016. http://www.pewsocialtrends.org/2016/05/24/for-first-time-in-modern-era-living-with-parents-edges-out-other-living-arrangements-for-18-to-34-year-olds/st_2016-05-24_young-adults-living-05/.

14   "Average salary for class of 2019 up almost 6 percent over class of 2018's." National Association of Colleges and Employers. 2020. https://www.naceweb.org.

15   "Percentage of Employers Offering Signing Bonuses Climbing." National Association of Colleges and Employers. 2018. https://www.naceweb.org.

16   Konrad, Matt. "Tuition Assistance: The Benefit That Boosts Retention." Scholarship America. 2019. https://scholarshipamerica.org/blog/tuition-assistance-the-secret-benefit-that-boosts-employee-retention/.

17   "2016 Human Capital Benchmarking Report." Society of Human Resource Management.

18   Ma, Jennifer, and Matea Pender. "Trends in College Pricing and Student Aid 2021." College Board Research. 2021. https://research.collegeboard.org/pdf/trends-college-pricing-student-aid-2021.pdf.

19   "2016 Human Capital Benchmarking Report." Society of Human Resource Management.

20   "College Is Just the Beginning." Georgetown University Center on Education and the Workforce. 2015. https://www.slideshare.net/CEWGeorgetown/20150203-training-memo-v8mc.

21   Ibid.

22   Ibid.

23   "Talent Investments Pay Off." Lumina Foundation. n.d. https://www.luminafoundation.org/files/resources/talent-investments-pay-off-cigna-executive-summary.pdf.

24   "Designing and Managing Educational Assistance Programs." Society of Human Resource Management. n.d. https://www.shrm.org/resourcesandtools/tools-and-samples/toolkits/pages/educationalassistanceprograms.aspx.

25   "State of the American Workplace." Gallup. 2017.

26   Chiwaya, Nigel. "These five charts show how bad the student loan debt situation is." NBC News. 2019. https://www.nbcnews.com/news/us-news/student-loan-statistics-2019-n997836.

27   Ibid.

28   "Tips for Launching a Student-Loan Repayment Benefit." Society of Human
     Resource Management. 2017. https://www.shrm.org/resourcesandtools/hr-topics/
     benefits/pages/launching-student-loan-repayment-benefit.aspx.

29   Grensing-Pophal, Lin. "Employers' Student Loan Assistance Tackles the College
     Debt Crisis." SHRM. 2021. https://www.shrm.org/resourcesandtools/hr-topics/
     benefits/pages/employers-student-loan-assistance-tackles-the-college-debt-crisis.
     aspx

30   Gurchiek, Kathy. "Free Food Is a Tasty Benefit at Some Companies." Society for
     Human Resource Management. August 16, 2019. https://www.shrm.org/hr-today/
     news/hr-news/pages/free-food-is-a-tasty-benefit-at-some-companies.aspx.

31   "Recruiting Internally and Externally." Society for Human Resource Management.
     n.d. https://www.shrm.org/resourcesandtools/tools-and-samples/toolkits/pages/
     recruitinginternallyandexternally.aspx.

32   Ibid.

33   Mann, Annamarie. "3 Ways You Are Failing Your Remote Workers." Gallup. 2017.
     http://news.gallup.com/opinion/gallup/214946/ways-failing-remote-workers.aspx.

34   Matos, Calinsky, and Bond. "National Study of Employers."

35   Lister, Kate. "2017 State of Telecommuting in the U.S. Employee Workforce".
     Global Workplace Analytics. 2017. https://globalworkplaceanalytics.com/white-
     papers.

36   Ibid.

37   Hirst, Peter, Justin Talbot, Leigh Marz, Nicholas Petrie, and Alice Boyes. "How a
     Flex-Time Program at MIT Improved Productivity, Resilience, and Trust." *Harvard
     Business Review*. 2016. https://hbr.org/2016/06/how-a-flex-time-program-at-mit-
     improved-productivity-resilience-and-trust.

38   Lister, Kate. "2017 State of Telecommuting in the U.S. Employee Workforce".

39   Ibid.

40   Ibid.

41   Ibid.

42   Gross, Andrew. "Nearly 80% of Drivers Express Significant Anger, Aggression or
     Road Rage." AAA Newsroom. 2016. http://newsroom.aaa.com/2016/07/nearly-
     80-percent-of-drivers-express-significant-anger-aggression-or-road-rage/.

43   Dvorak, Nate, Junko Sasaki, and Annamarie Mann. "Employees at Home: Less
     Engaged." Gallup Poll. 2017. https://news.gallup.com/businessjournal/207539/
     employees-home-less-engaged.aspx.

44   "Stress and decision-making during the pandemic." American Psychological
     Association. 2021. https://www.apa.org/news/press/releases/stress/2021/octo-
     ber-decision-making.

45 Duarte, Carrie, Bhushan Sethi, and Elizabeth Greenberg. "How to stay connected when working remotely." PwC. n.d. https://www.pwc.com/us/en/library/covid-19/how-to-stay-connected-working-remotely.html.

46 "Managing for Employee Retention." Society for Human Resource Management. https://www.shrm.org/resourcesandtools/tools-and-samples/toolkits/pages/managingforemployeeretention.aspx.

47 Nishizaki and DellaNeve. "National Survey of Gen Z at Work."

48 Sorenson, Susan. "How Employees' Strengths Make Your Company Stronger." Gallup Poll. 2014. https://news.gallup.com/businessjournal/167462/employees-strengths-company-stronger.aspx.

49 McLaren, Samantha. "Here's How IBM Predicts 95% of Its Turnover Using Data." LinkedIn. 2019. https://business.linkedin.com/talent-solutions/blog/artificial-intelligence/2019/IBM-predicts-95-percent-of-turnover-using-AI-and-data.

50 Middlesworth, Matt. "Is Job Rotation the Answer to Reducing Injury Risk?" Society for Human Resource Management. 2015. https://www.shrm.org/resourcesandtools/hr-topics/risk-management/pages/job-rotation-reducing-injury-risk.aspx.

51 "Managing for Employee Retention." Society for Human Resource Management.

52 Frey, William H., and Tonantzin Carmona. "The US will become 'minority white' in 2045, Census projects." Brookings Institution. 2018. https://www.brookings.edu/blog/the-avenue/2018/03/14/the-us-will-become-minority-white-in-2045-census-projects/.

53 Myers, Verna. "Diversity Doesn't Stick Without Inclusion." The Verna Myers Company. 2017. https://www.vernamyers.com/2017/02/04/diversity-doesnt-stick-without-inclusion/.

54 "Defining DEI." Office of Diversity, Equity & Inclusion. University of Michigan. n.d. https://diversity.umich.edu/about/defining-dei/.

55 Barroso, Amanda, and Brown, Anna. "Gender pay gap in U.S. held steady in 2020." Pew Research Center. 2021. https://www.pewresearch.org/fact-tank/2021/05/25/gender-pay-gap-facts/.

56 Krentz, Matt, Emily Kos, Anna Green, and Jennifer Garcia-Alonso. "Easing the COVID-19 Burden on Working Parents." Boston Consulting Group. 2020. https://www.bcg.com/en-us/publications/2020/helping-working-parents-ease-the-burden-of-covid-19.

57 Kenney, Lisa. "Companies Can't Ignore Shifting Gender Norms." *Harvard Business Review*. 2020. https://hbr.org/2020/04/companies-cant-ignore-shifting-gender-norms.

58 Ibid.

59 Sakurai, Shige. "How Do I Use Your Pronouns Correctly?" MyPronouns.org. n.d. https://www.mypronouns.org/how.

60 Frey, William H., and Tonantzin Carmona. "The US will become 'minority white' in 2045, Census projects." Brookings Institution. 2018. https://www.brookings.edu/blog/the-avenue/2018/03/14/the-us-will-become-minority-white-in-2045-census-projects/.

61 Parker, Kim, and Ruth Iglienk. "What We Know About Gen Z So Far." Pew Research Center. 2020. https://www.pewresearch.org/social-trends/2020/05/14/on-the-cusp-of-adulthood-and-facing-an-uncertain-future-what-we-know-about-gen-z-so-far-2/.

62 Hewlett, Sylvia A., Melinda Marshall, and Laura Sherbin. "How Diversity Can Drive Innovation." *Harvard Business Review*. 2013. https://hbr.org/2013/12/how-diversity-can-drive-innovation.

63 Sherbin, Laura, and Ripa Rashid. "Diversity Doesn't Stick Without Inclusion." *Harvard Business Review*. 2017. https://hbr.org/2017/02/diversity-doesnt-stick-without-inclusion.

64 Ibid.

65 Ibid.

66 Ibid.

67 Ibid.

68 Ibid.

69 "The role of diversity practices and inclusion in promoting trust and employee engagement." Deloitte. n.d. https://www2.deloitte.com/au/en/pages/human-capital/articles/role-diversity-practices-inclusion-trust-employee-engagement.html.

70 "Waiter, is that inclusion in my soup? A new recipe to improve business performance." Deloitte. 2013. https://www2.deloitte.com/content/dam/Deloitte/au/Documents/human-capital/deloitte-au-hc-diversity-inclusion-soup-0513.pdf.

71 Ibid.

72 Hewlett, Marshall, and Sherbin. "How Diversity Can Drive Innovation."

73 Sherbin and Rashid. "Diversity Doesn't Stick Without Inclusion."

74 Lorenzo, Rocio, Nicole Voigt, Miki Tsusaka, Matt Krentz, and Katie Abouzahr. "How Diverse Leadership Teams Boost Innovation." BCG Global. December 16, 2021. https://www.bcg.com/publications/2018/how-diverse-leadership-teams-boost-innovation.

75 Rock, David, and Heidi Grant. "Why Diverse Teams Are Smarter." *Harvard Business Review*. 2016. https://hbr.org/2016/11/why-diverse-teams-are-smarter.

76 Shook, Ellyn, and Julie Sweet. "Equality & Innovation in the Workplace." Accenture. n.d. https://www.accenture.com/_acnmedia/thought-leadership-assets/pdf/accenture-equality-equals-innovation-gender-equality-research-report-iwd-2019.pdf.

77 Krentz, Matt, Olivier Wierzba, Katie Abouzahr, Jennifer Garcia-Alonso, and Frances Brooks Taplett. "Five Ways Men Can Improve Gender Diversity at Work." Boston Consulting Group. 2017. https://www.bcg.com/publications/2017/people-organization-behavior-culture-five-ways-men-improve-gender-diversity-work.

FIVE

1 Indeed Editorial Team. "6 Different Work Environment Types and Example Career Roles." Indeed. 2021. https://www.indeed.com/career-advice/finding-a-job/different-work-environment-types.

2 Hickman, Adam, and Jennifer Robison. "5 Facts About Engagement and Remote Workers." Gallup. 2020. https://www.gallup.com/workplace/309521/facts-engagement-remote-workers.aspx.

3 Lister, Kate. "2017 State of Telecommuting in the U.S. Employee Workforce."

4 Barman, Tushar. "Future of office space post COVID." Deloitte. 2021. https://www2.deloitte.com/us/en/insights/topics/strategy/future-of-office-space-post-covid.html.

5 Hickman, Adam, and Jennifer Robison. "Is Working Remotely Effective." Gallup. 2020. https://www.gallup.com/workplace/283985/working-remotely-effective-gallup-research-says-yes.aspx.

6 Ibid.

7 "Global Millennial Survey 2020." Deloitte.

8 Hickman and Robison. "5 Facts About Engagement and Remote Workers."

9 "Global Millennial Survey 2020." Deloitte.

10 Ibid.

11 Maurer, Roy. "Study Finds Productivity Not Deterred by Shift to Remote Work." Society of Human Resource Management. 2020. https://www.shrm.org/hr-today/news/hr-news/pages/study-productivity-shift-remote-work-covid-coronavirus.aspx.

12 Dahik, Adriana, Deborah Lovich, Caroline Kreafle, Allison Bailey, Julie Kilmann, Derek Kennedy, Prateek Roongta, Felix Schuler, Leo Tomlin, and John Wenstrup. "What 12,000 Employees Have to Say About the Future of Remote Work." Boston Consulting Group. 2020. https://www.bcg.com/en-us/publications/2020/valuable-productivity-gains-covid-19.

13 "Global Millennial Survey 2020." Deloitte.

14 Parker, Sharon K., Caroline Knight, and Anita Keller. "Remote Managers Are Having Trust Issues." *Harvard Business Review*. 2020. https://hbr.org/2020/07/remote-managers-are-having-trust-issues.

15 Ibid.

16 "Global Millennial Survey 2020." Deloitte.

17   "Over 90% of Young Workers Having Difficulty Working from Home, Survey
     Finds." Smartsheet. 2020. https://www.smartsheet.com/content-center/news/over-
     90-young-workers-having-difficulty-working-home-survey-finds.

18   Fosslien, Lisa, and Mollie West Duffy. "How to Combat Zoom Fatigue." *Harvard
     Business Review*. 2020. https://hbr.org/2020/04/how-to-combat-zoom-fatigue.

19   "Millennials, Gen Z and Mental Health" Managing Mental Health in the
     Workplace." Deloitte. Accessed July 9, 2022. https://www2.deloitte.com/content/
     dam/Deloitte/global/Documents/About-Deloitte/gx-millennial-survey-men-
     tal-health-whitepaper.pdf.

20   "Global Millennial Survey 2020." Deloitte.

21   Geiger, A. W. "Most Americans say libraries can help them find reliable, trust-
     worthy information." Pew Research Center. 2017. https://www.pewresearch.
     org/fact-tank/2017/08/30/most-americans-especially-Millennials-say-librar-
     ies-can-help-them-find-reliable-trustworthy-information/.

22   Wilson, James. "The Surprising Power of Impulse Control." *Harvard Business
     Review*. 2014. https://hbr.org/2014/02/the-surprising-power-of-impulse-control.

23   Maurer, Roy. "How to Reduce Digital Distractions at Work." Society for Human
     Resource Management. 2019. https://www.shrm.org/ResourcesAndTools/hr-top-
     ics/technology/Pages/Reducing-Digital-Distractions-at-Work.aspx.

24   "6 Companies That Have Taken Bold Stands on Social Issues." JUST Capital.
     2019. https://justcapital.com/news/companies-that-have-taken-bold-stands-on-
     social-issues/.

25   Vogels, Emily A., Monica Anderson, Margaret Porteus, Chris Baronavski, Sara
     Atske, Colleen McClain, Brooke Auxier, Andrew Perrin, and Meera Ramshankar.
     "Americans and 'Cancel Culture': Where Some See Calls for Accountability,
     Others See Censorship, Punishment." Pew Research Center. 2021. https://
     www.pewresearch.org/internet/2021/05/19/americans-and-cancel-cul-
     ture-where-some-see-calls-for-accountability-others-see-censorship-punishment/.

26   Brenner, Grant H. "The Psychology of Cancel Culture and Mass Violence Risk."
     Psychology Today. 2020. https://www.psychologytoday.com/us/blog/experimenta-
     tions/202006/large-group-psychology-racism-and-cancel-culture.

27   Brenner, Grant H. "Gen Z and Workplace Bullying, Ghosting, and Cancel
     Culture." *Psychology Today*. 2021. https://www.psychologytoday.com/us/blog/
     experimentations/202107/gen-z-and-workplace-bullying-ghosting-and-cancel-
     culture.

28   Ibid.

29   Twenge, Jean M. "The Smartphone Generation vs. Free Speech." *Wall Street
     Journal*. 2017. https://www.wsj.com/articles/the-smartphone-generation-vs-free-
     speech-1504274890.

30   Bauer, Jeremy. "Study: students believe they are prepared for the workplace; employers disagree." Inside Higher Ed. 2018. https://www.insidehighered.com/news/2018/02/23/study-students-believe-they-are-prepared-workplace-employers-disagree.

31   "Managing Workplace Conflict." Society for Human Resource Management. n.d. https://www.shrm.org/resourcesandtools/tools-and-samples/toolkits/pages/managingworkplaceconflict.aspx.

32   Gallo, Amy. *HBR Guide to Dealing with Conflict.* Harvard Business Review Press. 2017.

33   Ibid.

34   Nagele, Lisa. "Workplace Bullying and Harassment: What's the Difference?" Society for Human Resource Management. 2018. https://www.shrm.org/resourcesandtools/legal-and-compliance/state-and-local-updates/pages/workplace-bullying.aspx.

35   Anderson, Monica, and Colleen McClain, Michelle Faverio, and Risa Gelles-Watnick. "The State of Gig Work in 2021." Pew Research Center. 2021. https://www.pewresearch.org/internet/2021/12/08/the-state-of-gig-work-in-2021/36 "Job Outlook 2018 Survey." National Association of Colleges and Employers. Retrieved from: https://www.insidehighered.com/news/2018/02/23/study-students-believe-they-are-prepared-workplace-employers-disagree.

SIX

1   "State of the American Workplace." Gallup. 2017.

2   Simon, Tim. "How the Best Managers Break 'The Golden Rule' Every Day." Gallup. 2018. http://coaching.gallup.com/2018/03/manage-by-exception-not-golden-rule.html?utm_source=coachingblog&utm_medium=LinkedIn&utm_campaign=socialmedia.

3   "Set Your New Managers up for Success: Developing New Leaders." Center for Creative Leadership. December 7, 2021. https://www.ccl.org/articles/leading-effectively-articles/prepare-first-time-leaders-success/.

4   Northouse, Peter G. *Leadership: Theory and Practice.* Thousand Oaks, CA: SAGE Publications, 2018.

5   Ibid.

6   Ibid.

7   Beck, Randall, and Jim Harter. "Managers Account for 70% of Variance in Employee Engagement." Gallup News. 2015. https://news.gallup.com/businessjournal/182792/managers-account-variance-employee-engagement.aspx.

8   "State of the American Manager." Gallup. n.d. http://www.gallup.com/services/182138/state-american-manager.aspx.

9   McLeod, Saul. "Maslow's Hierarchy of Needs." Simply Psychology. 2020. https://www.simplypsychology.org/maslow.html.

10 Hirsch, Arlene S. "Don't Underestimate the Importance of Good Onboarding." Society for Human Resource Management. 2017. https://www.shrm.org/resourcesandtools/hr-topics/talent-acquisition/pages/dont-underestimate-the-importance-of-effective-onboarding.aspx.

11 Meinert, Dori. "Onboarding Mistakes to Avoid And Some Creative Ideas to Adopt." Society for Human Resource Management. n.d. https://www.shrm.org/hr-today/news/hr-magazine/0616/pages/onboarding-mistakes-to-avoid-and-some-creative-ideas-to-adopt.aspx.

12 Robison, Jennifer. "Give Up Bossing, Take Up Coaching: You'll Like the Results." Gallup. 2020. https://www.gallup.com/workplace/282647/give-bossing-coaching-results.aspx.

13 Ibarra, Herminia, and Anne Scoular. "The Leader as Coach." *Harvard Business Review*. 2019. https://hbr.org/2019/11/the-leader-as-coach.

14 Fuller, Ryan, and Nina Shikaloff. "What Great Managers Do Daily." *Harvard Business Review*. 2016. https://hbr.org/2016/12/what-great-managers-do-daily.

15 Lencioni, Patrick. "Five Dysfunctions Products." The Table Group. n.d. https://www.tablegroup.com/books/dysfunctions/.

16 Kaplan, Robert S., and David P. Norton. "Using the Balanced Scorecard as a Strategic Management System." *Harvard Business Review*. 2007. https://hbr.org/2007/07/using-the-balanced-scorecard-as-a-strategic-management-system.

17 "8 Ways To Build Workplace Relationships." Indeed. 2021. https://www.indeed.com/career-advice/career-development/how-to-build-relationships.

18 Ibid.

19 George, Bill, and Peter Sims. *Authentic Leadership: Rediscovering the Secrets to Creating Lasting Value*. Hoboken, NJ: John Wiley & Sons, 2004.

20 "22. Bring Your Full Self to Work." Toyota USA Newsroom. 2019. https://pressroom.toyota.com/podcast/22-bring-your-full-self-to-work/.

21 Brim, Brian J. "Strengths-Based Leadership: The 4 Things Followers Need." Gallup. May 23, 2022. https://www.gallup.com/cliftonstrengths/en/251003/strengths-based-leadership-things-followers-need.aspx.

22 Lazzaroni Pate, Deanna. "The Top Skills In Demand For 2020—And How to Learn Them." LinkedIn. 2020. https://www.linkedin.com/business/learning/blog/top-skills-and-courses/the-skills-companies-need-most-in-2020and-how-to-learn-them.

23 D'Onfro, Jillian. "The Truth About Google's Famous '20% Time' Policy." Business Insider. 2015. https://www.businessinsider.com/google-20-percent-time-policy-2015-4.

24 Govindarajan, Vijay. "Innovation Is Not Creativity." *Harvard Business Review.* 2010. https://hbr.org/2010/08/innovation-is-not-creativity.html.

25 Deloitte. "Millennials a Catalyst for Innovation." *Wall Street Journal.* n.d. https://deloitte.wsj.com/articles/Millennials-a-catalyst-for-innovation-1396324924?tesla=y.

26 Govindarajan. "Innovation Is Not Creativity."

27 Sherbin and Rashid. "Diversity Doesn't Stick Without Inclusion."

28 Caglar, Deniz, Vinay Couto, Ed Faccio, and Bhushan Sethi. "It's time to reimagine where and how work will get done—US Remote Work Survey." Pricewaterhouse-Coopers. 2021. https://www.pwc.com/us/en/library/covid-19/us-remote-work-survey.html.

29 Ibid.

30 Ibid.

31 Romansky, Lauren, Mia Garrod, Katie Brown, and Kartik Deo. "How to Measure Inclusion in the Workplace." *Harvard Business Review.* 2021. https://hbr.org/2021/05/how-to-measure-inclusion-in-the-workplace.

32 RoAne, Susan. "How to Bring out the Best in Introverts." Society for Human Resource Management. 2017. https://www.shrm.org/resourcesandtools/hr-topics/employee-relations/pages/how-to-bring-out-the-best-in-introverts-.aspx.

33 Riggio, Ronald E. "5 Reasons Why Micromanagers Fail." *Psychology Today.* 2018. https://www.psychologytoday.com/us/blog/cutting-edge-leadership/201808/5-reasons-why-micromanagers-fail.

34 Wigert, Ben, and Ryan Pendell. "The Ultimate Guide to Micromanagers: Signs, Causes, Solutions." Gallup. 2020. https://www.gallup.com/workplace/315530/ultimate-guide-micromanagers-signs-causes-solutions.aspx.

35 Northouse. *Leadership.*

36 Goleman, Daniel. "Leadership That Gets Results." *Harvard Business Review.* 2000. https://hbr.org/2000/03/leadership-that-gets-results.

37 Northouse. *Leadership.*

38 Ibid.

CLOSING THOUGHTS

1 Jones, Jeffrey M. "U.S. Church Membership Falls below Majority for First Time." Gallup. November 20, 2021. https://news.gallup.com/poll/341963/church-membership-falls-below-majority-first-time.aspx.

ACKNOWLEDGMENTS

There are so many amazing people who helped bring this project to life. First, we would like to thank Amplify Publishing, which helped support us every step of the way. We want to thank our writing coach, Kris Drewry-Perelmutter, who gave us great feedback and tips when we needed it most. Also, we'd like to thank our project manager at Amplify, Brandon Coward, who helped us stay on track and get our book to the finish line. Thank you, Paul Epstein, for introducing us to Amplify and its CEO, Naren Aryal. Our thanks also go to Destiny Calderon, who did the detailed work of getting permissions for the large volume of research material. We would have been lost without her! Next, we'd like to thank Jonathan Arnold, who helped us review contracts.

We want to thank Paul Allen, founder of Ancestry.com, and his daughter, who devoted precious time to writing our foreword while growing his fantastic company, Soar. Next, we'd like to thank Dr. Grant Brenner, whom we had the opportunity to interview for this book and eventually collaborate with on a couple of *Psychology Today* articles as well as a future study and book. Also, we'd like to thank Dr. Doreen Dodgen-Magee, PsyD, (author of *Deviced!* and *Restart*) and Dr. David Greenfield (author of *Overcoming Internet Addiction for Dummies*) for their incredible wisdom and knowledge about how to create meaningful connections at home and work.

SANTOR

First, I would like to thank my family: Katia, Thomas, and Jamie. We started this project in 2017. Since then, there have been many phone calls and Zoom meetings that took me away from them in order to tell the story of this remarkable generation. Next, I would like to thank my fantastic coauthor, James, who was on the other end of the phone and Zoom calls with me and devoted countless hours to working on this project. He has become a great friend of mine and will be for years to come.

Next, I'd like to thank one of my mentors, Dr. Paul Sabolic, who supported me from day one and had no problem reminding me every time we met that the book wasn't finished. After almost six years, I can finally hand him a copy! Also, I'd like to thank another one of my mentors, Craig Russell, who has been supportive of my career since I left Disney and is always willing to help.

I want to thank Maggie Harris—who has been with me on my journey since I decided to start my company and write this book—for taking the time to review it and provide helpful tips. Finally, I'd like to thank Conner Krizancic, my amazing CMO, for offering great feedback since we started working together and for creating one of the graphics in the book.

JAMES

I would like to thank my family: Fay, Paul, Vanessa, and Noelle. They always cheered and inquired about our progress on this journey. And they were there for me when I would have writer's block or become submerged in research and need to come up for air. Next, I would like to thank Santor, a truly amazing man. His energy, enthusiasm, intellect, and drive were invaluable for this project. I've come to appreciate his friendship and wonderful family.

I also want to thank others with whom I have partnered in my Gen Z experiences. I have served on the board of Alta Loma Christian School (ALCS) as well as assisted with starting their award-winning STEM program with Dr. Vance Nichols, the head of school. I have also served ALCS with Pastor Mike Collins. My discussions with Vance and Mike about my research findings have been invaluable. I used these two great men as a sounding board and a litmus test for the research. I'd also like to thank the amazing and energetic Pat Sandoval. Pat led the high school intern program at Boeing's satellite development program. I was able to work with Pat and the Gen Z interns for many years. Santor and I were able to run workshops with the Gen Zers and compare our research with their experiences. These workshops were invaluable in terms of verifying our research.

I love the resulting book and the work that went into it—from the design to the style of writing to all the editing—to get a good product out there. I think that this book is useful and timely.